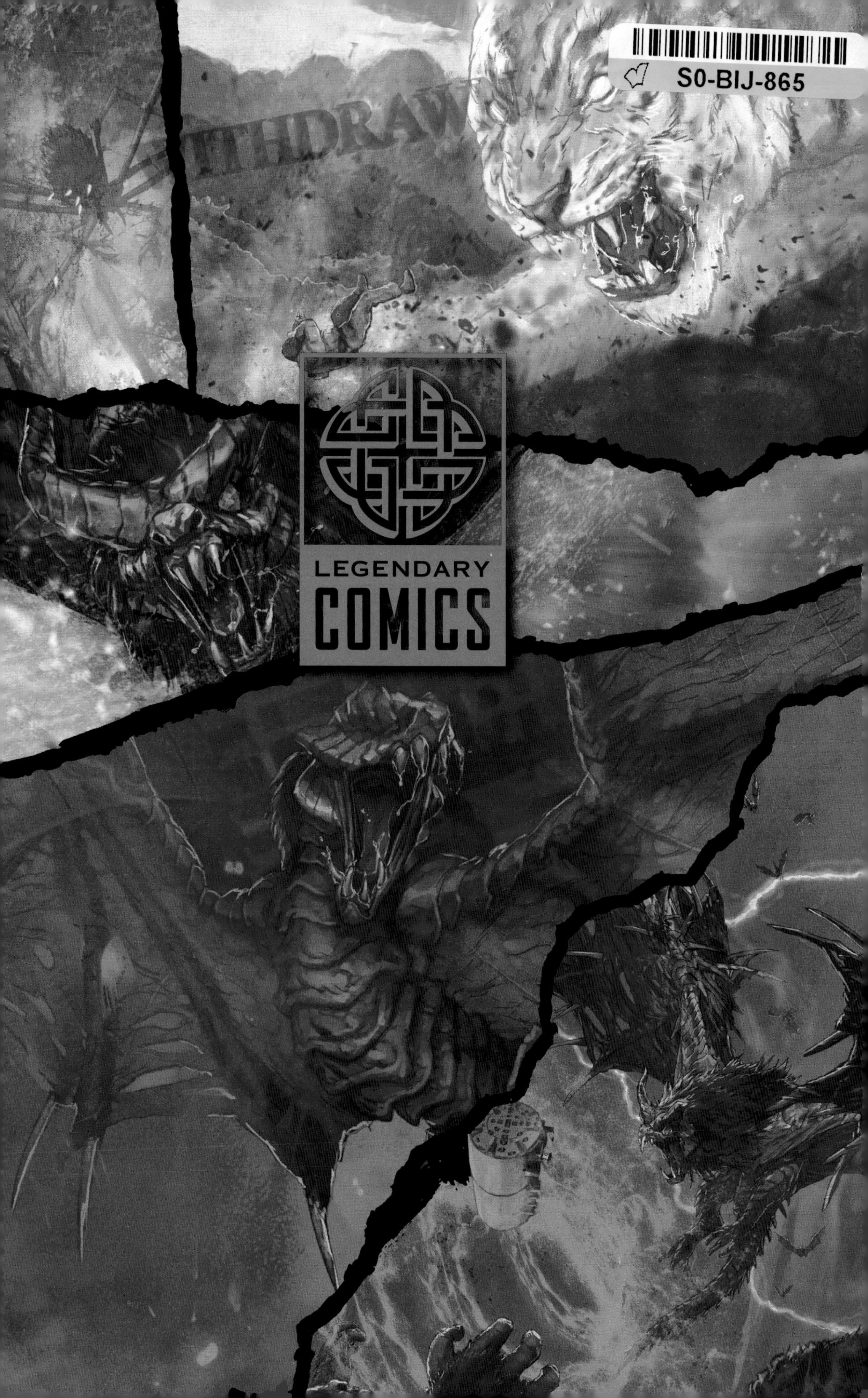
LEGENDARY
COMICS

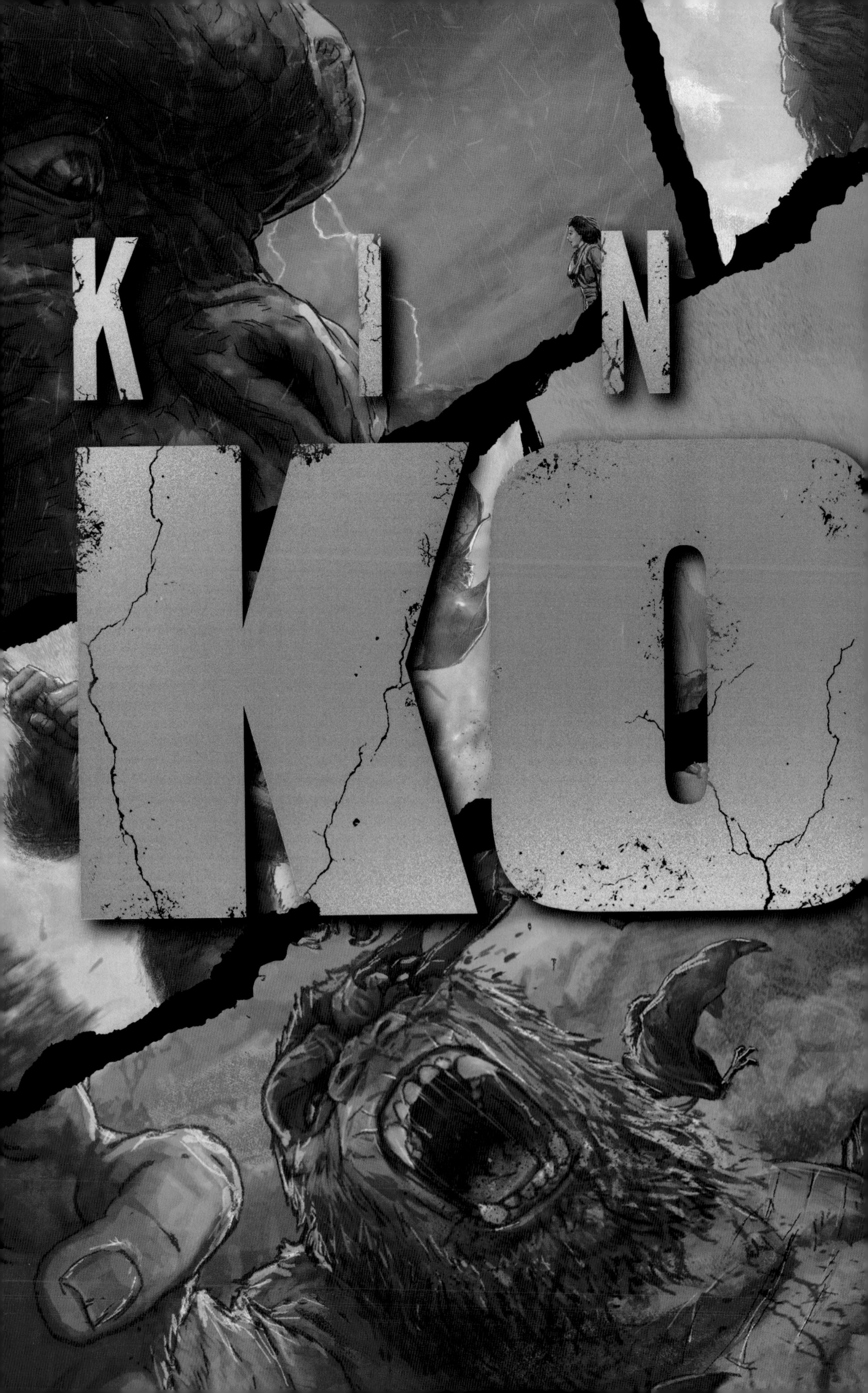
KIN
KO

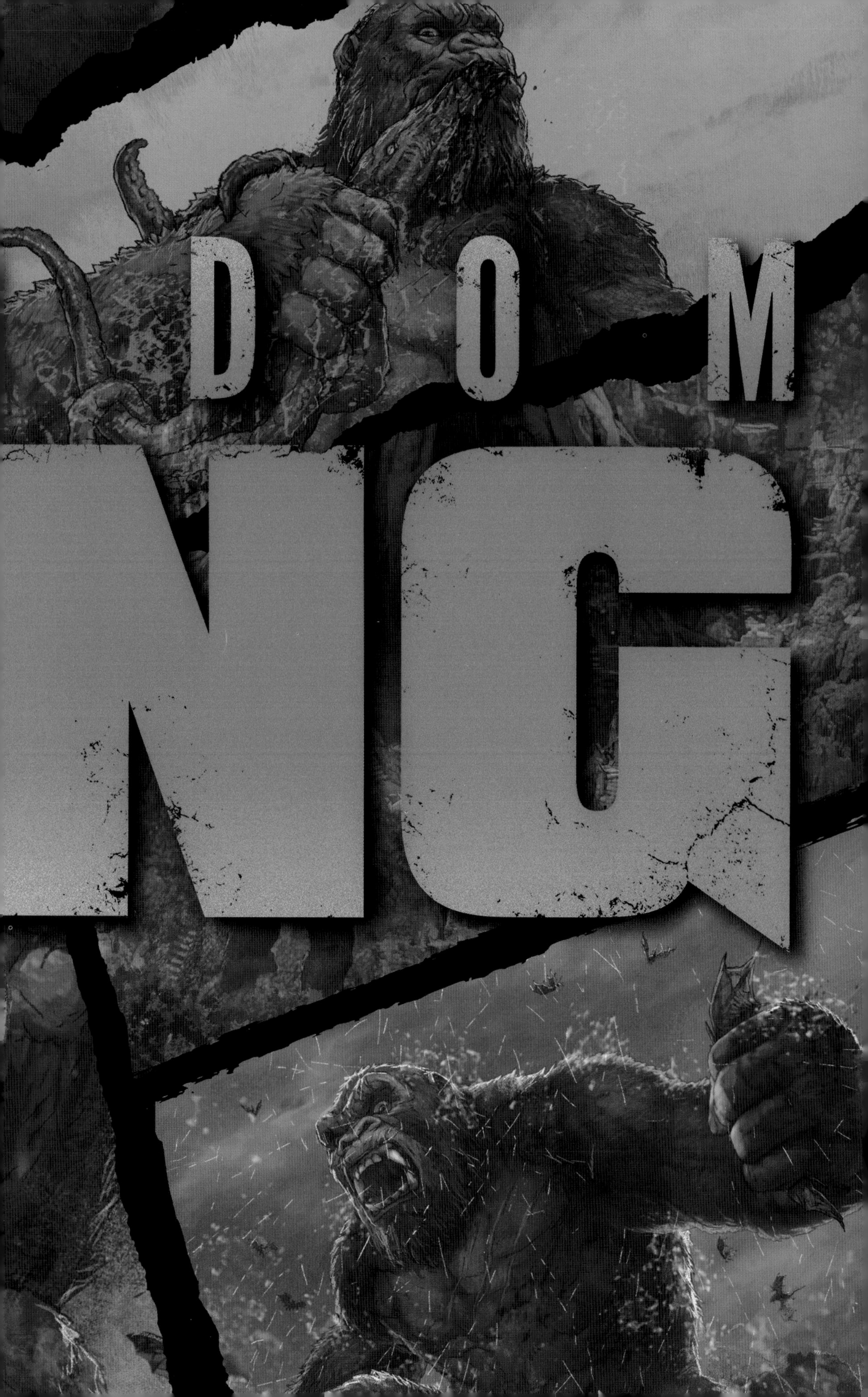
DOM
NG

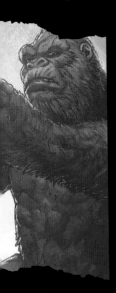

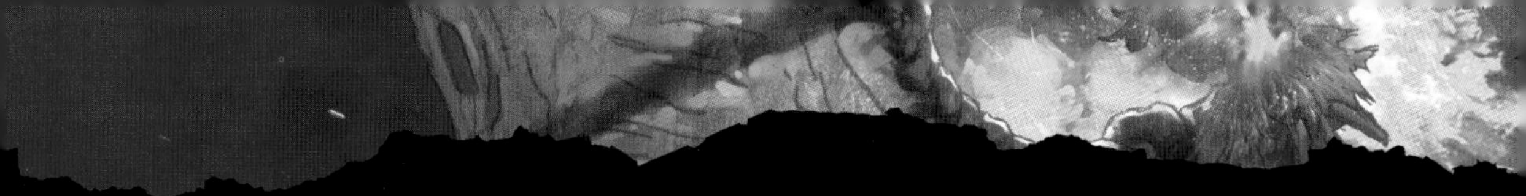

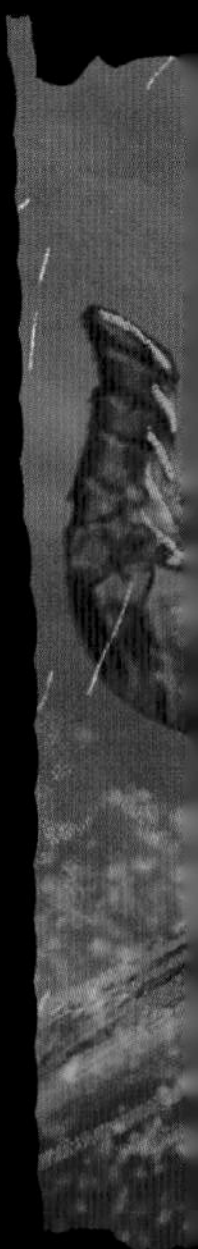

MARIE ANELLO
Writer

ARTHUR ADAMS
Cover

ZID
Art

SYNCRAFT STUDIO
Color Assists

RICHARD STARKINGS & COMICRAFT

JIMMY BETANCOURT
Lettering

TYLER SMITH
Design

ROBERT NAPTON & NIKITA KANNEKANTI
Editors

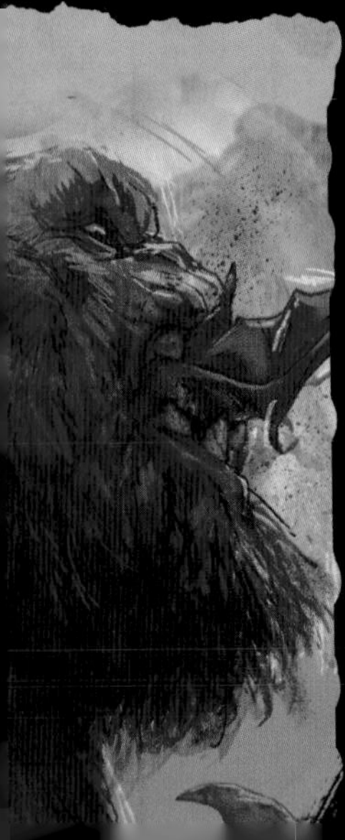

BARNABY LEGG
Story and Mythology Development

JOSH PARKER
KATIE AGUILAR
BRIAN HOFFMAN
Monsterverse Creative

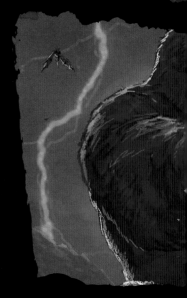

Alex Garcia
Jay Ashenfelter
Zak Kline
Brooke Hansohn
George Tew
Makenna Knudson
Jennifer Stewart
Sarah Jarvis
Tracy Brown
Brie Dorsey
Legendary Legal
Legendary Marketing
Spencer Douglas

Special Thanks

LEGENDARY

JOSHUA GRODE
Chief Executive Officer

MARY PARENT
Vice Chairman of Worldwide Production

CHRIS ALBRECHT
Managing Director, Legendary Television

RONALD HOHAUSER
Chief Financial Officer

BARNABY LEGG
SVP, Creative Strategy

MIKE ROSS
EVP, Business & Legal Affairs

KRISTINA HOLLIMAN
SVP, Business & Legal Affairs

BAYAN LAIRD
SVP, Business & Legal Affairs

LEGENDARY COMICS

ROBERT NAPTON SVP, Publishing • **NIKITA KANNEKANTI** Editor
JANN JONES Manager, Brand Development & Publishing Operations

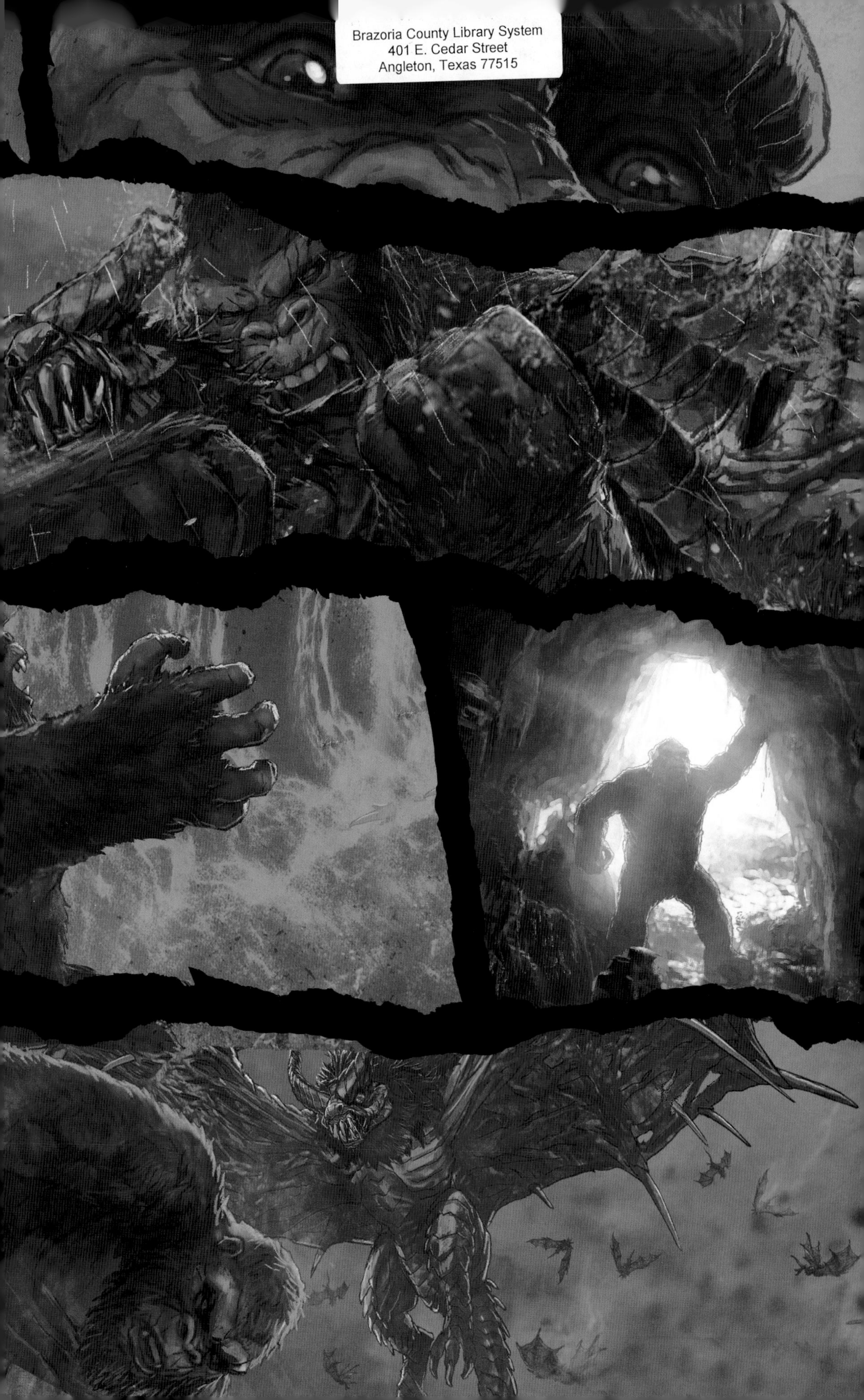

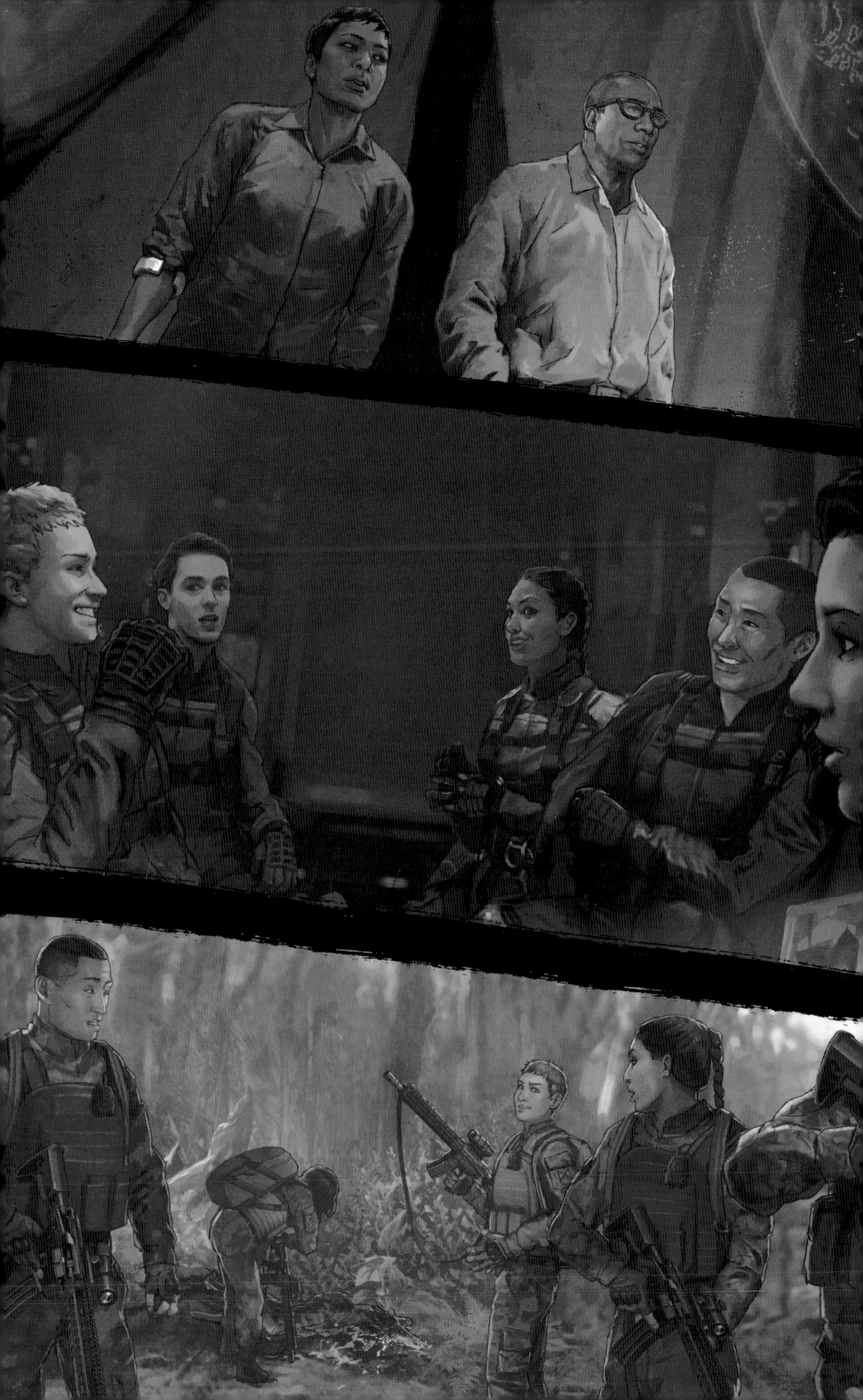

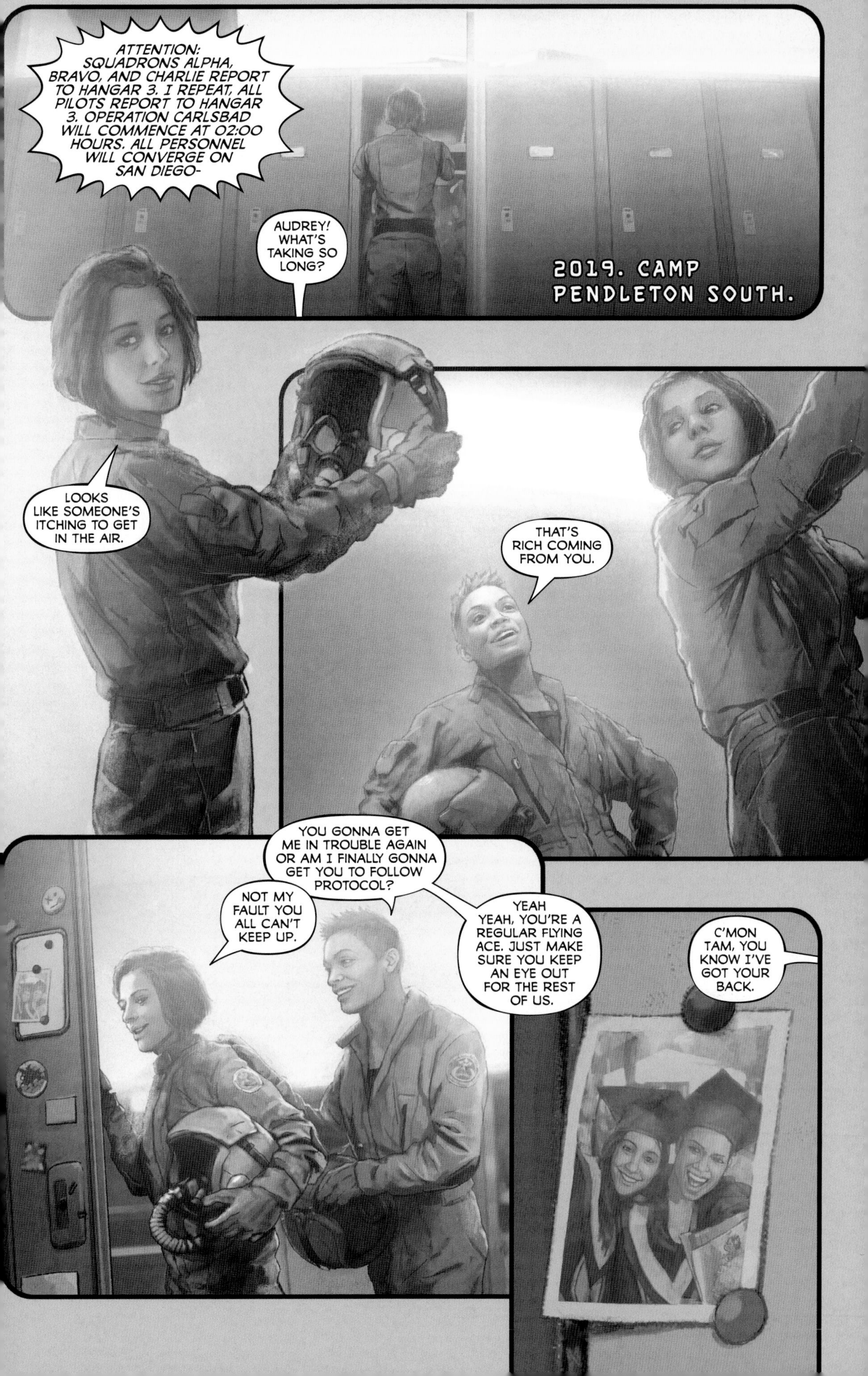
ATTENTION: SQUADRONS ALPHA, BRAVO, AND CHARLIE REPORT TO HANGAR 3. I REPEAT, ALL PILOTS REPORT TO HANGAR 3. OPERATION CARLSBAD WILL COMMENCE AT 02:00 HOURS. ALL PERSONNEL WILL CONVERGE ON SAN DIEGO-
AUDREY! WHAT'S TAKING SO LONG?
2019. CAMP PENDLETON SOUTH.
LOOKS LIKE SOMEONE'S ITCHING TO GET IN THE AIR.
THAT'S RICH COMING FROM YOU.
YOU GONNA GET ME IN TROUBLE AGAIN OR AM I FINALLY GONNA GET YOU TO FOLLOW PROTOCOL?
NOT MY FAULT YOU ALL CAN'T KEEP UP.
YEAH YEAH, YOU'RE A REGULAR FLYING ACE. JUST MAKE SURE YOU KEEP AN EYE OUT FOR THE REST OF US.
C'MON TAM, YOU KNOW I'VE GOT YOUR BACK.

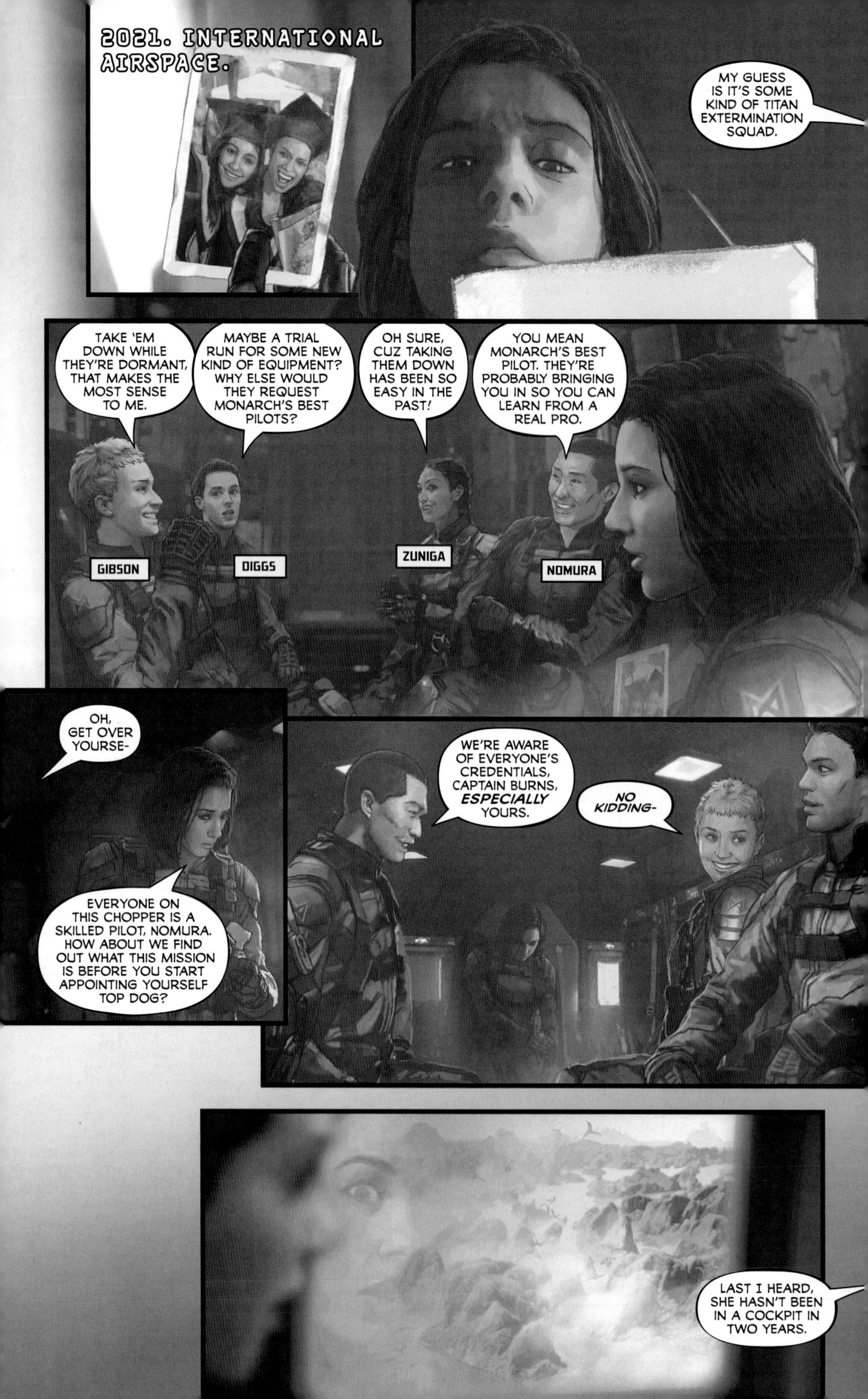
2021. INTERNATIONAL AIRSPACE.
MY GUESS IS IT'S SOME KIND OF TITAN EXTERMINATION SQUAD.
TAKE 'EM DOWN WHILE THEY'RE DORMANT, THAT MAKES THE MOST SENSE TO ME.
MAYBE A TRIAL RUN FOR SOME NEW KIND OF EQUIPMENT? WHY ELSE WOULD THEY REQUEST MONARCH'S BEST PILOTS?
OH SURE, CUZ TAKING THEM DOWN HAS BEEN SO EASY IN THE PAST!
YOU MEAN MONARCH'S BEST PILOT. THEY'RE PROBABLY BRINGING YOU IN SO YOU CAN LEARN FROM A REAL PRO.
GIBSON
DIGGS
ZUNIGA
NOMURA
OH, GET OVER YOURSE-
EVERYONE ON THIS CHOPPER IS A SKILLED PILOT, NOMURA. HOW ABOUT WE FIND OUT WHAT THIS MISSION IS BEFORE YOU START APPOINTING YOURSELF TOP DOG?
WE'RE AWARE OF EVERYONE'S CREDENTIALS, CAPTAIN BURNS, *ESPECIALLY* YOURS.
NO KIDDING-
LAST I HEARD, SHE HASN'T BEEN IN A COCKPIT IN TWO YEARS.

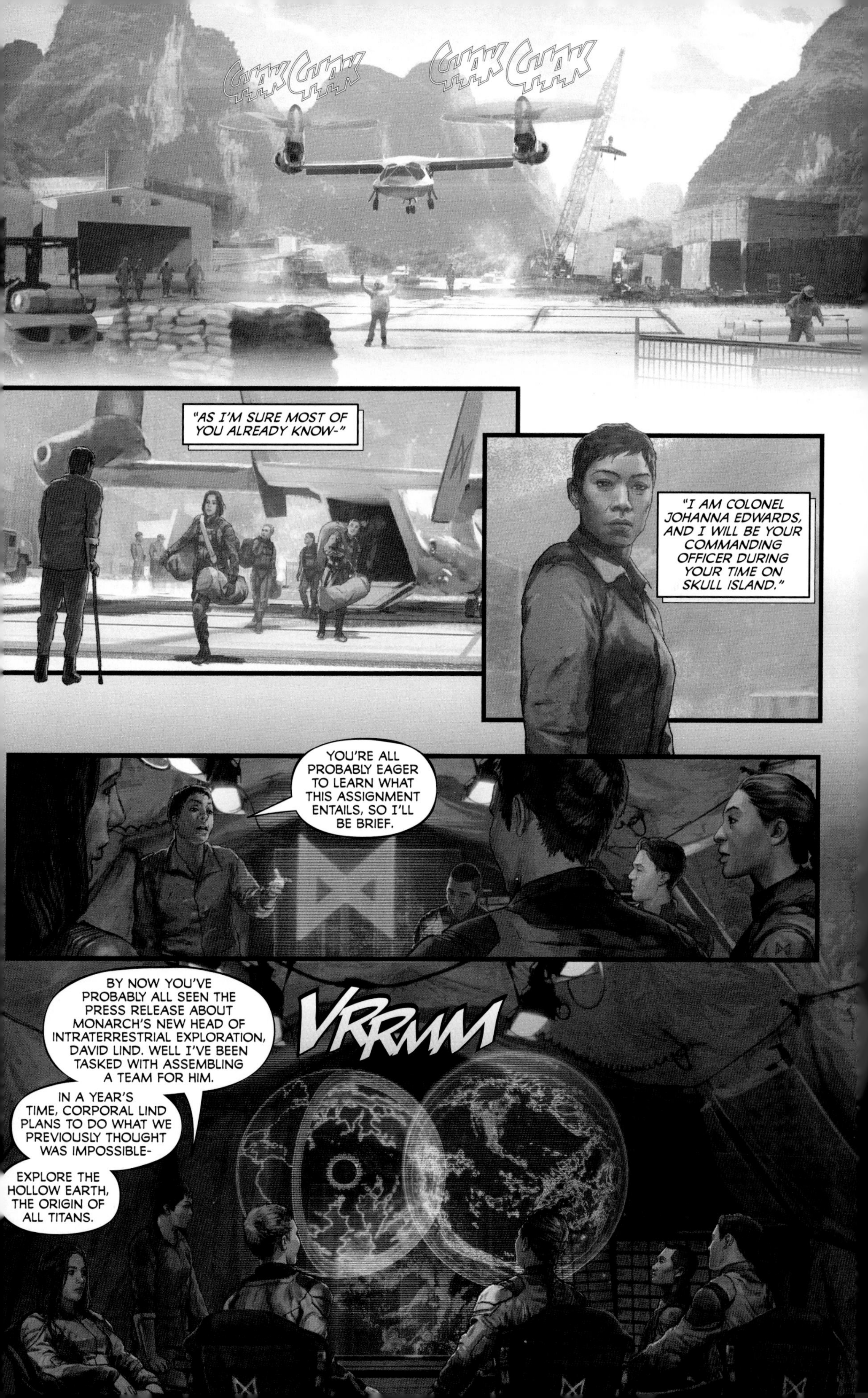
CHAK CHAK
CHAK CHAK
"AS I'M SURE MOST OF YOU ALREADY KNOW-"
"I AM COLONEL JOHANNA EDWARDS, AND I WILL BE YOUR COMMANDING OFFICER DURING YOUR TIME ON SKULL ISLAND."
YOU'RE ALL PROBABLY EAGER TO LEARN WHAT THIS ASSIGNMENT ENTAILS, SO I'LL BE BRIEF.
BY NOW YOU'VE PROBABLY ALL SEEN THE PRESS RELEASE ABOUT MONARCH'S NEW HEAD OF INTRATERRESTRIAL EXPLORATION, DAVID LIND. WELL I'VE BEEN TASKED WITH ASSEMBLING A TEAM FOR HIM.
IN A YEAR'S TIME, CORPORAL LIND PLANS TO DO WHAT WE PREVIOUSLY THOUGHT WAS IMPOSSIBLE-
EXPLORE THE HOLLOW EARTH, THE ORIGIN OF ALL TITANS.
VRRMM

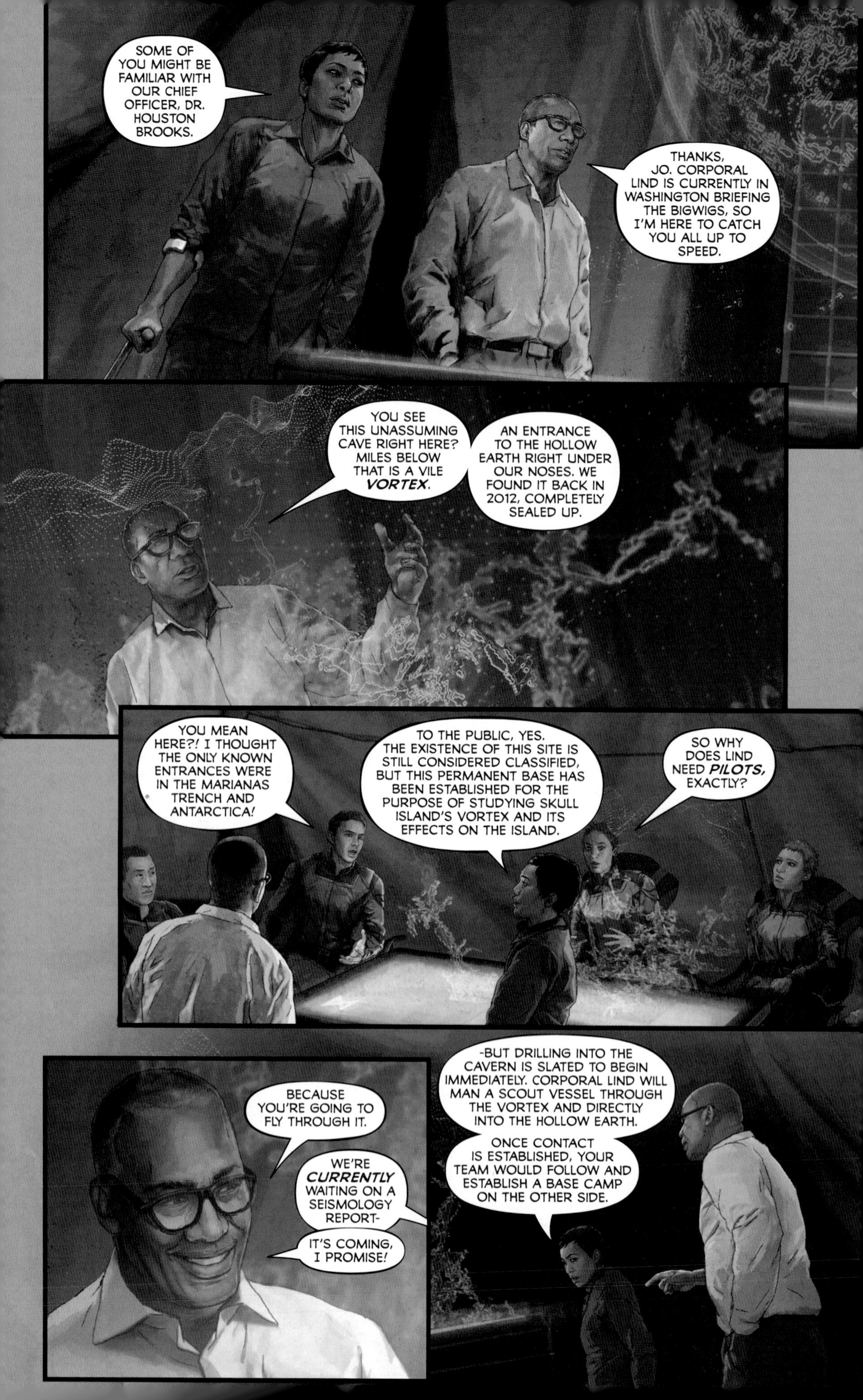
SOME OF YOU MIGHT BE FAMILIAR WITH OUR CHIEF OFFICER, DR. HOUSTON BROOKS.
THANKS, JO. CORPORAL LIND IS CURRENTLY IN WASHINGTON BRIEFING THE BIGWIGS, SO I'M HERE TO CATCH YOU ALL UP TO SPEED.
YOU SEE THIS UNASSUMING CAVE RIGHT HERE? MILES BELOW THAT IS A VILE VORTEX.
AN ENTRANCE TO THE HOLLOW EARTH RIGHT UNDER OUR NOSES. WE FOUND IT BACK IN 2012, COMPLETELY SEALED UP.
YOU MEAN HERE?! I THOUGHT THE ONLY KNOWN ENTRANCES WERE IN THE MARIANAS TRENCH AND ANTARCTICA!
TO THE PUBLIC, YES. THE EXISTENCE OF THIS SITE IS STILL CONSIDERED CLASSIFIED, BUT THIS PERMANENT BASE HAS BEEN ESTABLISHED FOR THE PURPOSE OF STUDYING SKULL ISLAND'S VORTEX AND ITS EFFECTS ON THE ISLAND.
SO WHY DOES LIND NEED PILOTS, EXACTLY?
BECAUSE YOU'RE GOING TO FLY THROUGH IT.
WE'RE CURRENTLY WAITING ON A SEISMOLOGY REPORT-
IT'S COMING, I PROMISE!
-BUT DRILLING INTO THE CAVERN IS SLATED TO BEGIN IMMEDIATELY. CORPORAL LIND WILL MAN A SCOUT VESSEL THROUGH THE VORTEX AND DIRECTLY INTO THE HOLLOW EARTH.
ONCE CONTACT IS ESTABLISHED, YOUR TEAM WOULD FOLLOW AND ESTABLISH A BASE CAMP ON THE OTHER SIDE.

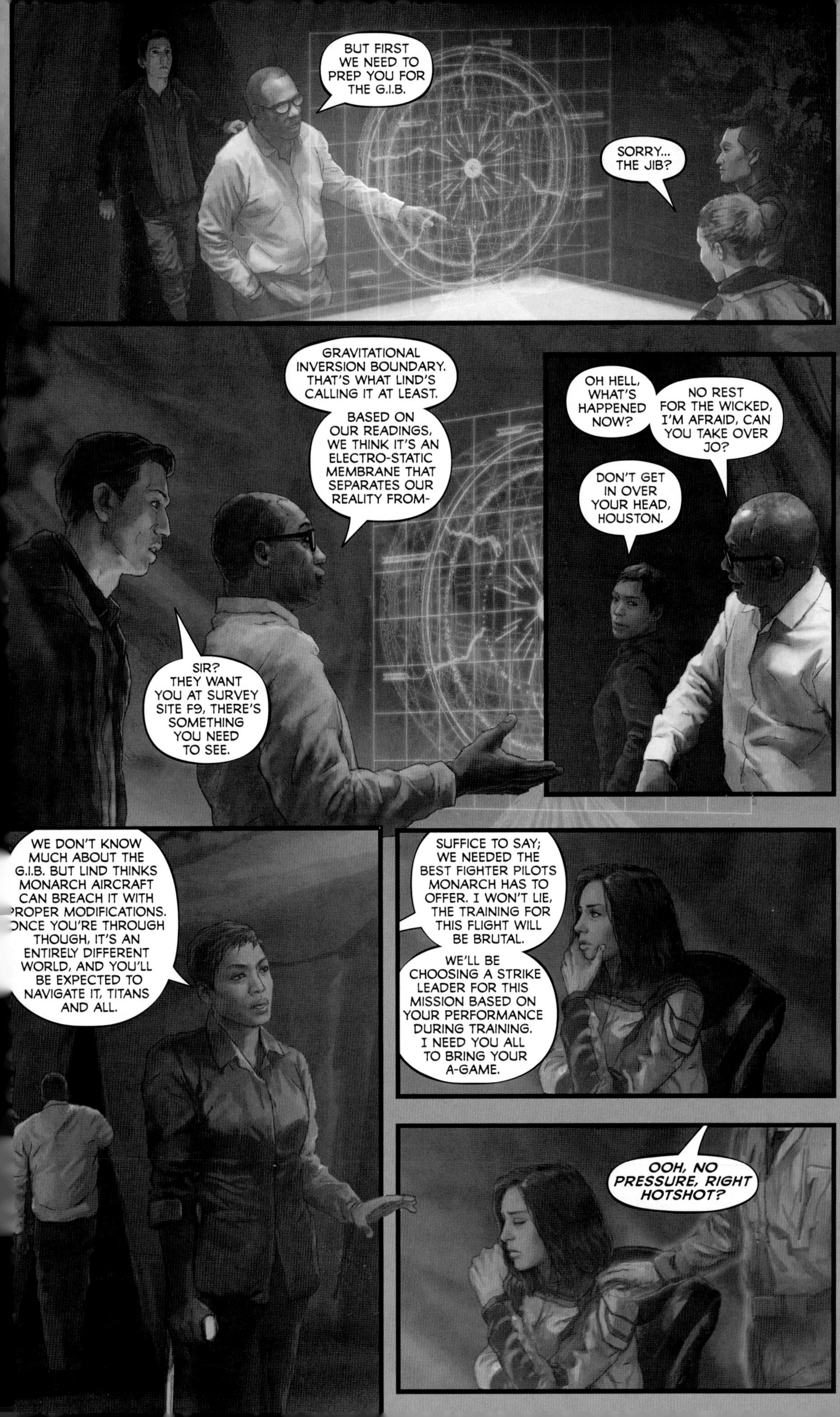

BUT FIRST WE NEED TO PREP YOU FOR THE G.I.B.
SORRY... THE JIB?
GRAVITATIONAL INVERSION BOUNDARY. THAT'S WHAT LIND'S CALLING IT AT LEAST.
BASED ON OUR READINGS, WE THINK IT'S AN ELECTRO-STATIC MEMBRANE THAT SEPARATES OUR REALITY FROM-
SIR? THEY WANT YOU AT SURVEY SITE F9, THERE'S SOMETHING YOU NEED TO SEE.
OH HELL, WHAT'S HAPPENED NOW?
NO REST FOR THE WICKED, I'M AFRAID, CAN YOU TAKE OVER JO?
DON'T GET IN OVER YOUR HEAD, HOUSTON.
WE DON'T KNOW MUCH ABOUT THE G.I.B. BUT LIND THINKS MONARCH AIRCRAFT CAN BREACH IT WITH PROPER MODIFICATIONS. ONCE YOU'RE THROUGH THOUGH, IT'S AN ENTIRELY DIFFERENT WORLD, AND YOU'LL BE EXPECTED TO NAVIGATE IT, TITANS AND ALL.
SUFFICE TO SAY; WE NEEDED THE BEST FIGHTER PILOTS MONARCH HAS TO OFFER. I WON'T LIE, THE TRAINING FOR THIS FLIGHT WILL BE BRUTAL.
WE'LL BE CHOOSING A STRIKE LEADER FOR THIS MISSION BASED ON YOUR PERFORMANCE DURING TRAINING. I NEED YOU ALL TO BRING YOUR A-GAME.
OOH, NO PRESSURE, RIGHT HOTSHOT?

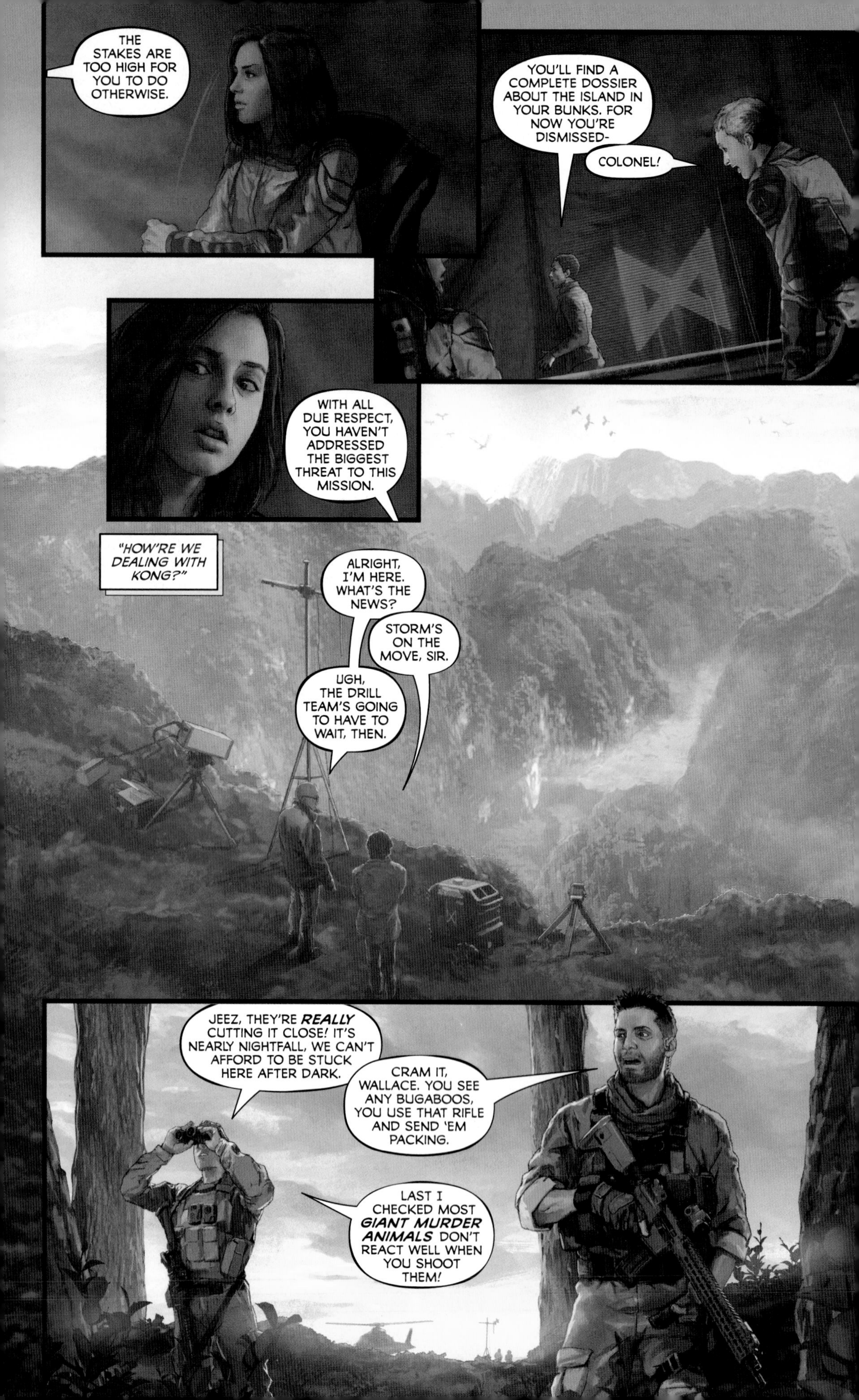

THE STAKES ARE TOO HIGH FOR YOU TO DO OTHERWISE.
YOU'LL FIND A COMPLETE DOSSIER ABOUT THE ISLAND IN YOUR BUNKS. FOR NOW YOU'RE DISMISSED-
COLONEL!
WITH ALL DUE RESPECT, YOU HAVEN'T ADDRESSED THE BIGGEST THREAT TO THIS MISSION.
"HOW'RE WE DEALING WITH KONG?"
ALRIGHT, I'M HERE. WHAT'S THE NEWS?
STORM'S ON THE MOVE, SIR.
UGH, THE DRILL TEAM'S GOING TO HAVE TO WAIT, THEN.
JEEZ, THEY'RE ***REALLY*** CUTTING IT CLOSE! IT'S NEARLY NIGHTFALL, WE CAN'T AFFORD TO BE STUCK HERE AFTER DARK.
CRAM IT, WALLACE. YOU SEE ANY BUGABOOS, YOU USE THAT RIFLE AND SEND 'EM PACKING.
LAST I CHECKED MOST ***GIANT MURDER ANIMALS*** DON'T REACT WELL WHEN YOU SHOOT THEM!

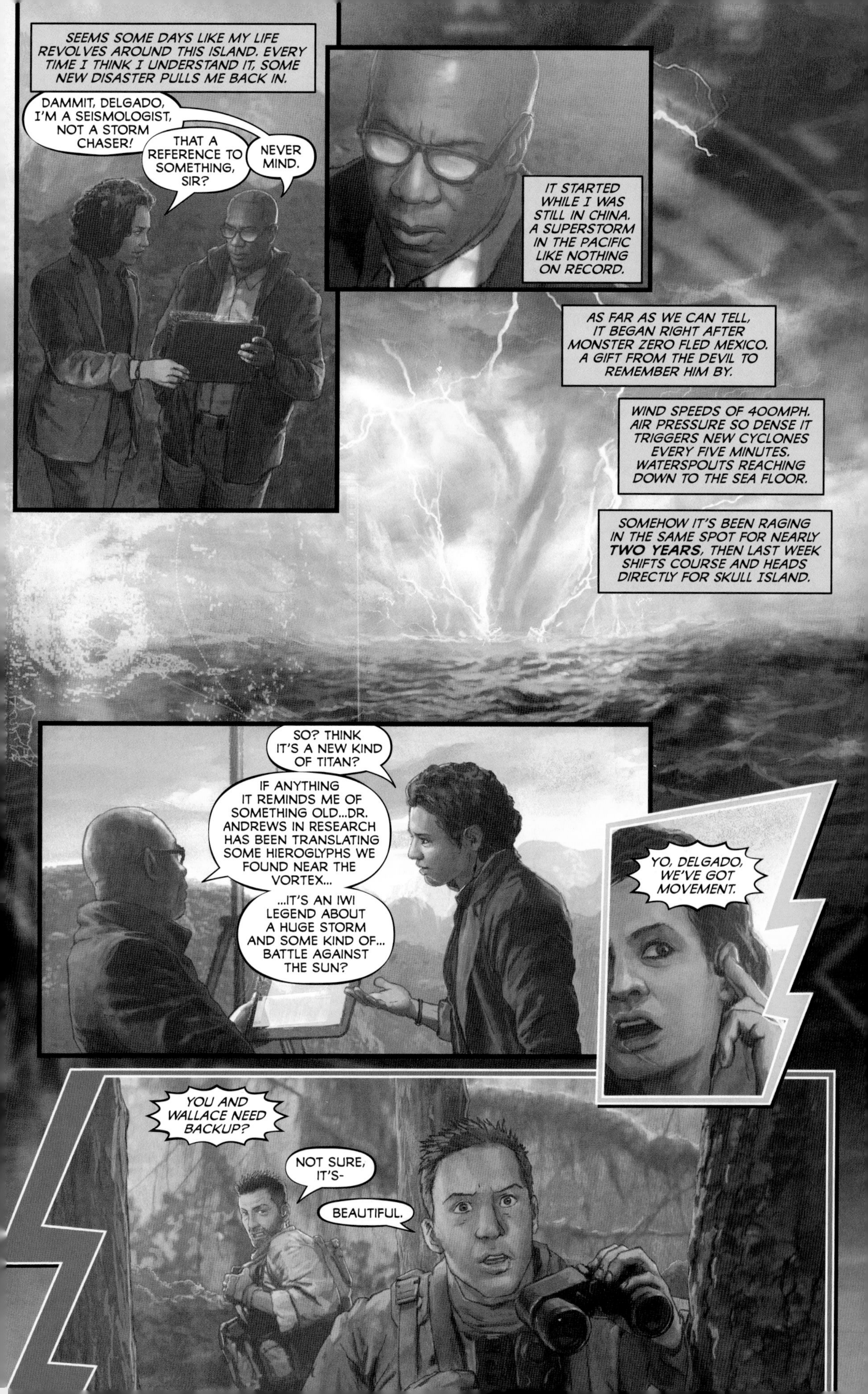
SEEMS SOME DAYS LIKE MY LIFE REVOLVES AROUND THIS ISLAND. EVERY TIME I THINK I UNDERSTAND IT, SOME NEW DISASTER PULLS ME BACK IN.
DAMMIT, DELGADO, I'M A SEISMOLOGIST, NOT A STORM CHASER!
THAT A REFERENCE TO SOMETHING, SIR?
NEVER MIND.
IT STARTED WHILE I WAS STILL IN CHINA. A SUPERSTORM IN THE PACIFIC LIKE NOTHING ON RECORD.
AS FAR AS WE CAN TELL, IT BEGAN RIGHT AFTER MONSTER ZERO FLED MEXICO. A GIFT FROM THE DEVIL TO REMEMBER HIM BY.
WIND SPEEDS OF 400MPH. AIR PRESSURE SO DENSE IT TRIGGERS NEW CYCLONES EVERY FIVE MINUTES. WATERSPOUTS REACHING DOWN TO THE SEA FLOOR.
SOMEHOW IT'S BEEN RAGING IN THE SAME SPOT FOR NEARLY TWO YEARS, THEN LAST WEEK SHIFTS COURSE AND HEADS DIRECTLY FOR SKULL ISLAND.
SO? THINK IT'S A NEW KIND OF TITAN?
IF ANYTHING IT REMINDS ME OF SOMETHING OLD...DR. ANDREWS IN RESEARCH HAS BEEN TRANSLATING SOME HIEROGLYPHS WE FOUND NEAR THE VORTEX...
...IT'S AN IWI LEGEND ABOUT A HUGE STORM AND SOME KIND OF... BATTLE AGAINST THE SUN?
YO, DELGADO, WE'VE GOT MOVEMENT.
YOU AND WALLACE NEED BACKUP?
NOT SURE, IT'S-
BEAUTIFUL.

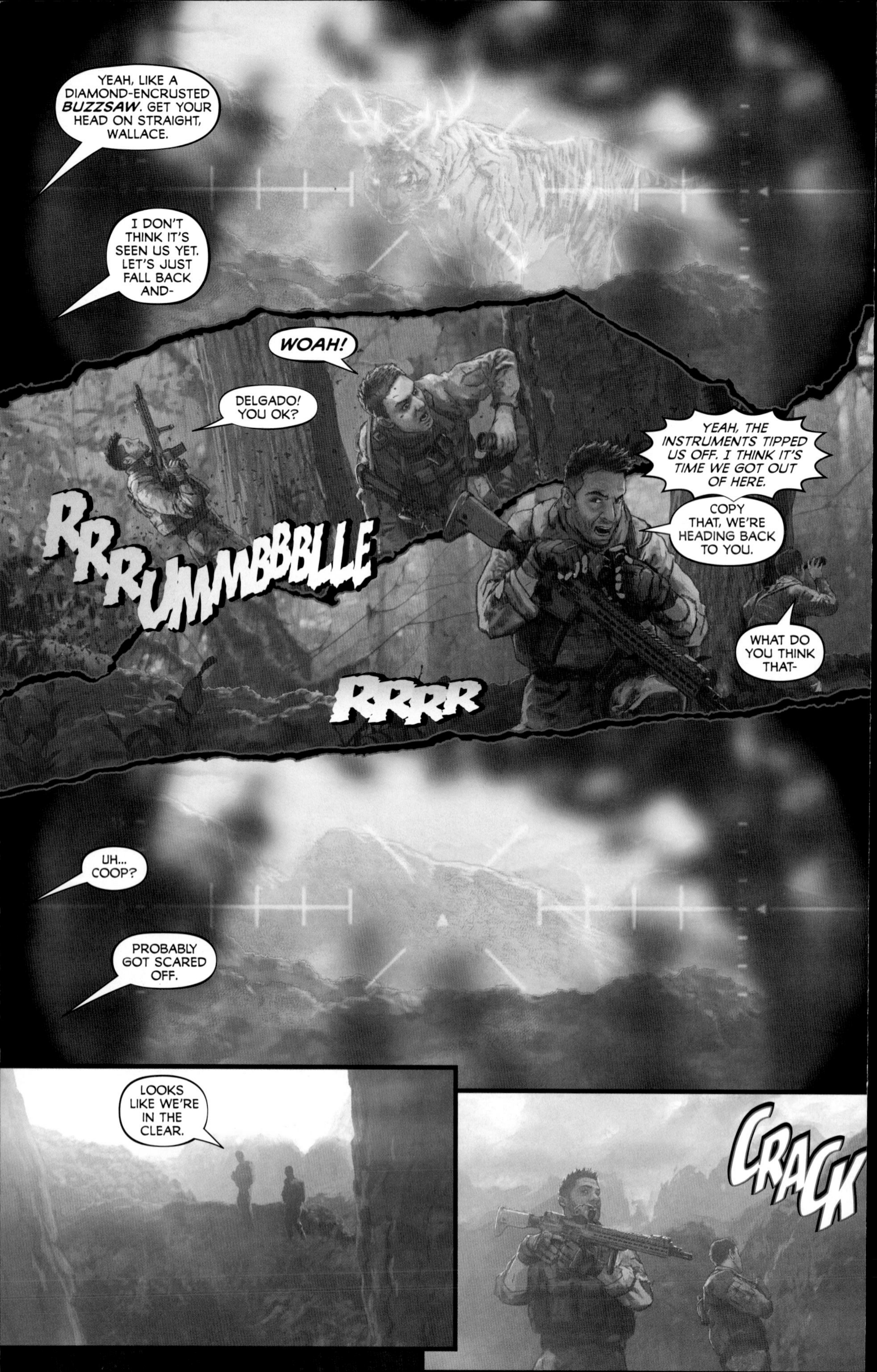

YEAH, LIKE A DIAMOND-ENCRUSTED BUZZSAW. GET YOUR HEAD ON STRAIGHT, WALLACE.
I DON'T THINK IT'S SEEN US YET. LET'S JUST FALL BACK AND-
WOAH!
DELGADO! YOU OK?
RRRUMMBBBLLE
YEAH, THE INSTRUMENTS TIPPED US OFF. I THINK IT'S TIME WE GOT OUT OF HERE.
COPY THAT, WE'RE HEADING BACK TO YOU.
WHAT DO YOU THINK THAT-
RRRR
UH... COOP?
PROBABLY GOT SCARED OFF.
LOOKS LIKE WE'RE IN THE CLEAR.
CRACK

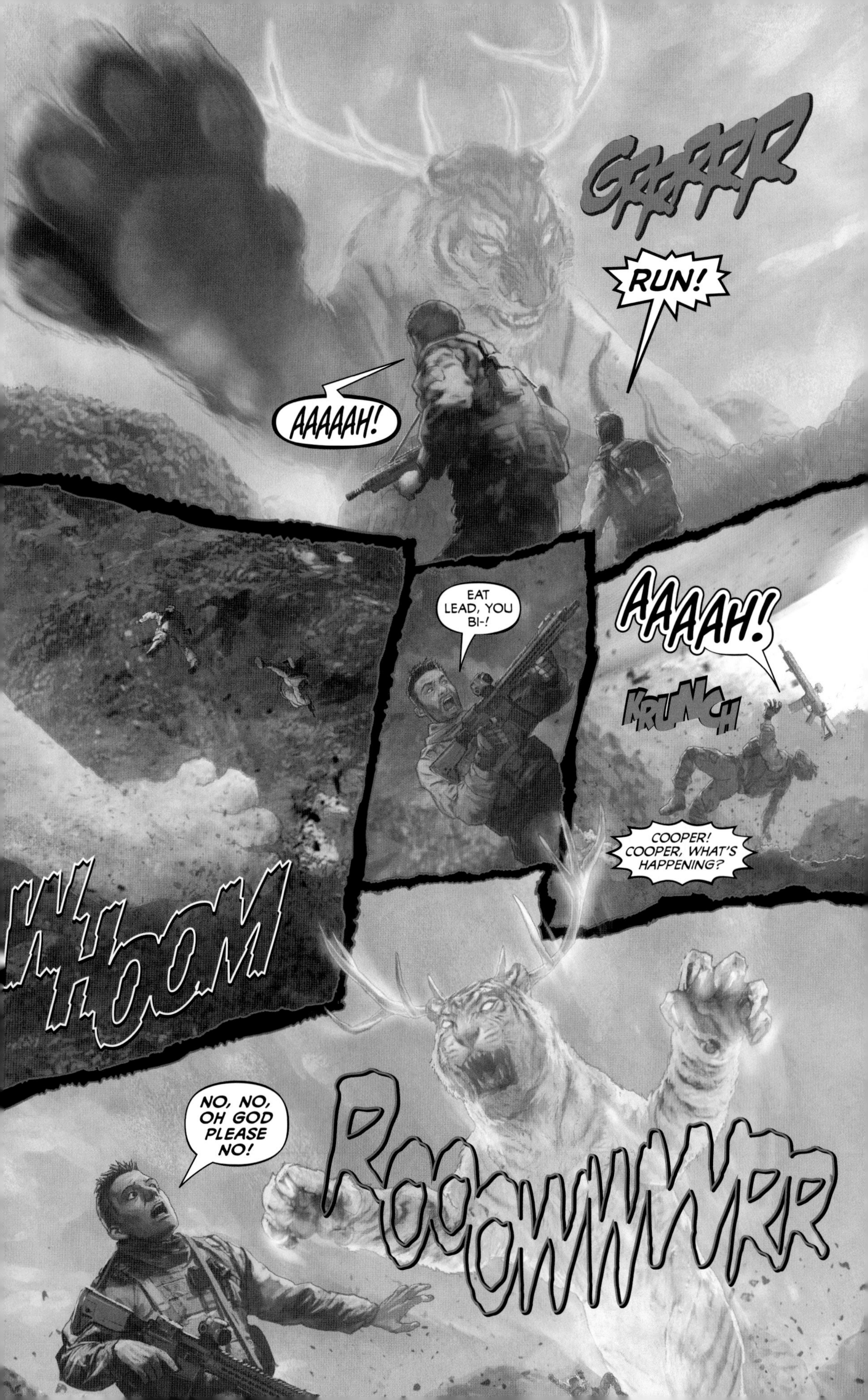
GRRRR
RUN!
AAAAAH!
EAT LEAD, YOU BI-!
AAAAH!
KRUNCH
COOPER! COOPER, WHAT'S HAPPENING?
WHOOM
NO, NO, OH GOD PLEASE NO!
ROOOWWWRR

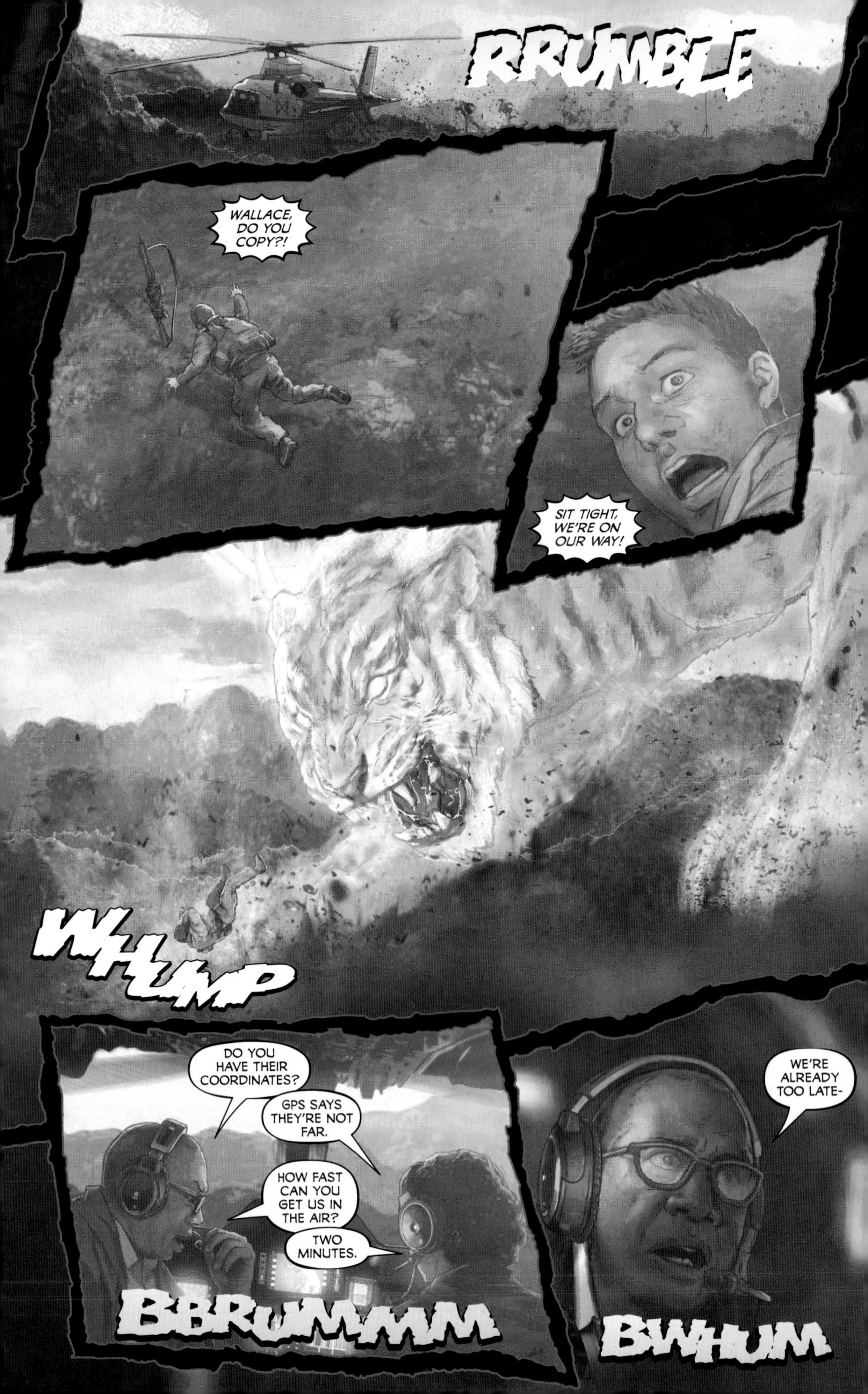
RRUMBLE
WALLACE, DO YOU COPY?!
SIT TIGHT, WE'RE ON OUR WAY!
WHUMP
DO YOU HAVE THEIR COORDINATES?
GPS SAYS THEY'RE NOT FAR.
HOW FAST CAN YOU GET US IN THE AIR?
TWO MINUTES.
BBRUMMM
WE'RE ALREADY TOO LATE-
BWHUM

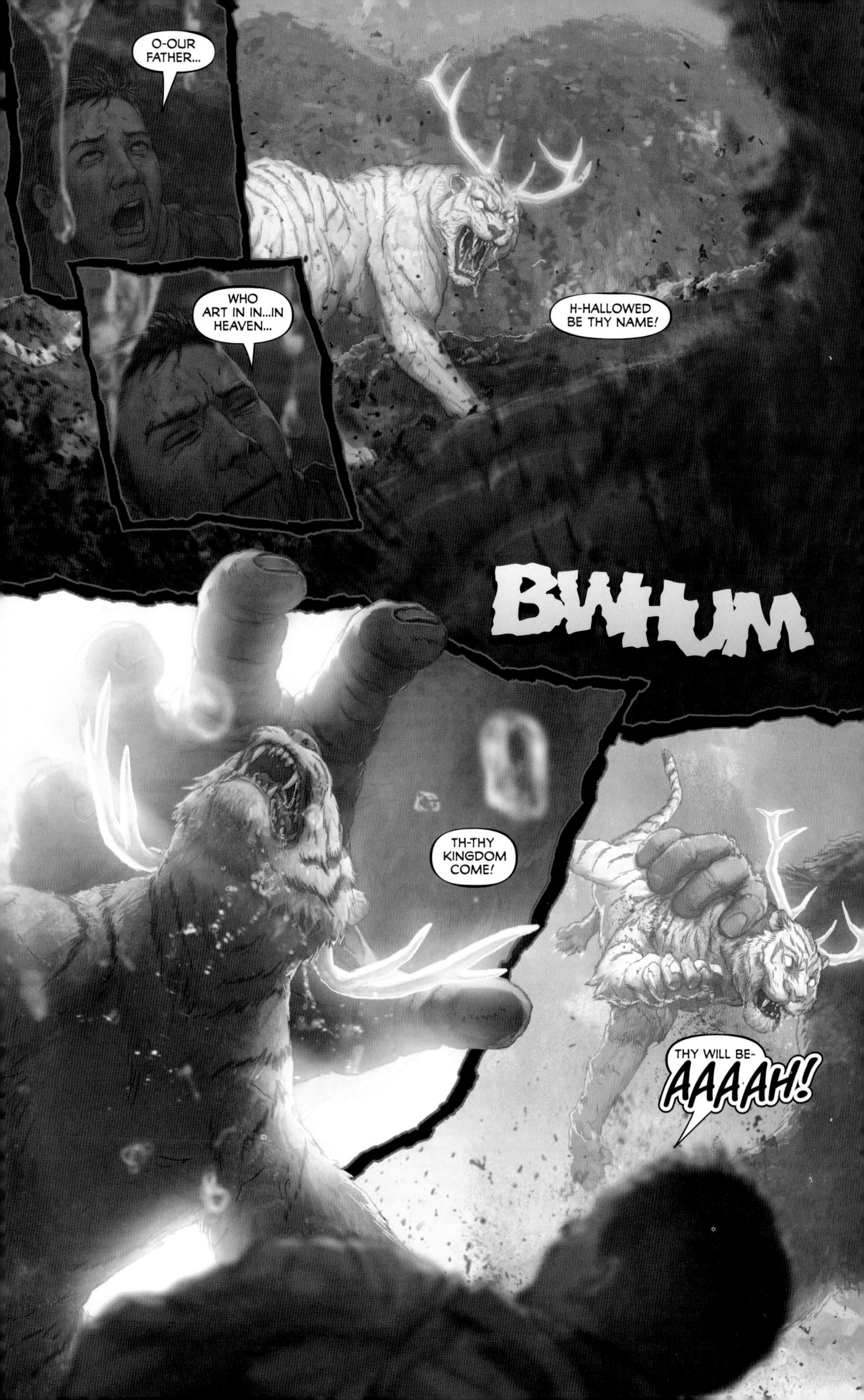
O-OUR FATHER...
WHO ART IN IN...IN HEAVEN...
H-HALLOWED BE THY NAME!
BWHUM
TH-THY KINGDOM COME!
THY WILL BE-
AAAAH!

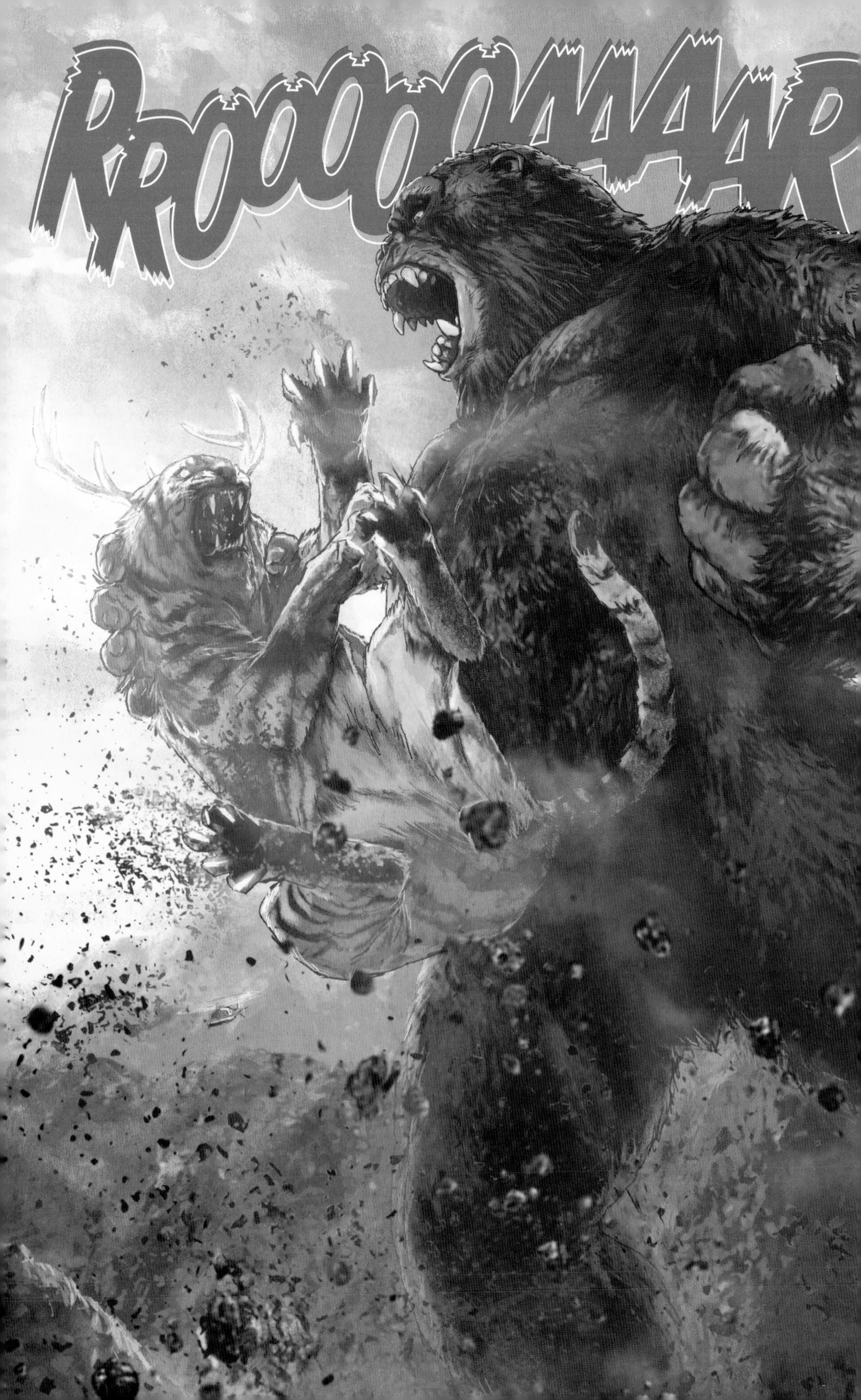
RROOOOOAAAR

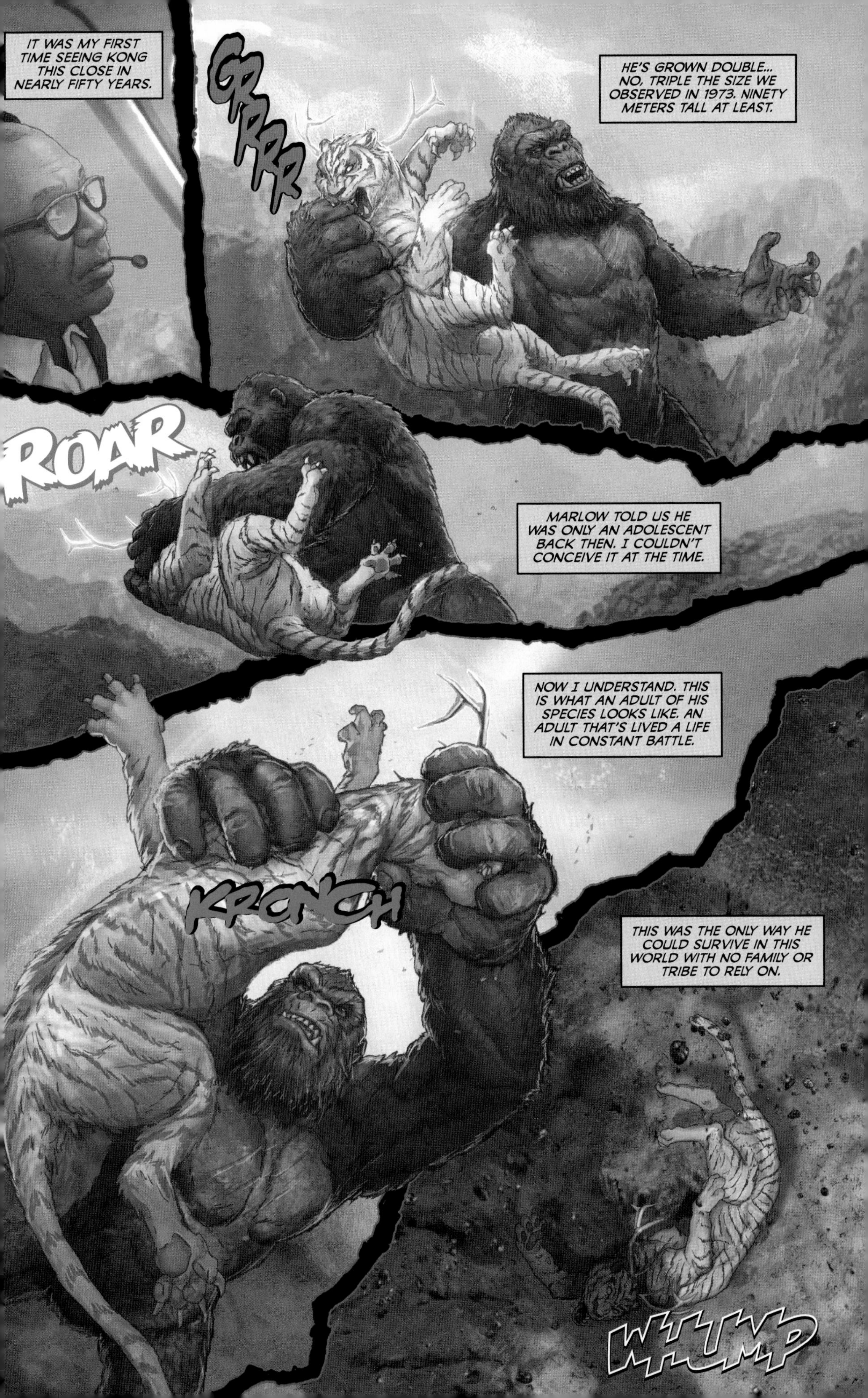
IT WAS MY FIRST TIME SEEING KONG THIS CLOSE IN NEARLY FIFTY YEARS.
GRRRR
HE'S GROWN DOUBLE... NO, TRIPLE THE SIZE WE OBSERVED IN 1973. NINETY METERS TALL AT LEAST.
ROAR
MARLOW TOLD US HE WAS ONLY AN ADOLESCENT BACK THEN. I COULDN'T CONCEIVE IT AT THE TIME.
NOW I UNDERSTAND. THIS IS WHAT AN ADULT OF HIS SPECIES LOOKS LIKE. AN ADULT THAT'S LIVED A LIFE IN CONSTANT BATTLE.
KRONCH
THIS WAS THE ONLY WAY HE COULD SURVIVE IN THIS WORLD WITH NO FAMILY OR TRIBE TO RELY ON.
WHUMP

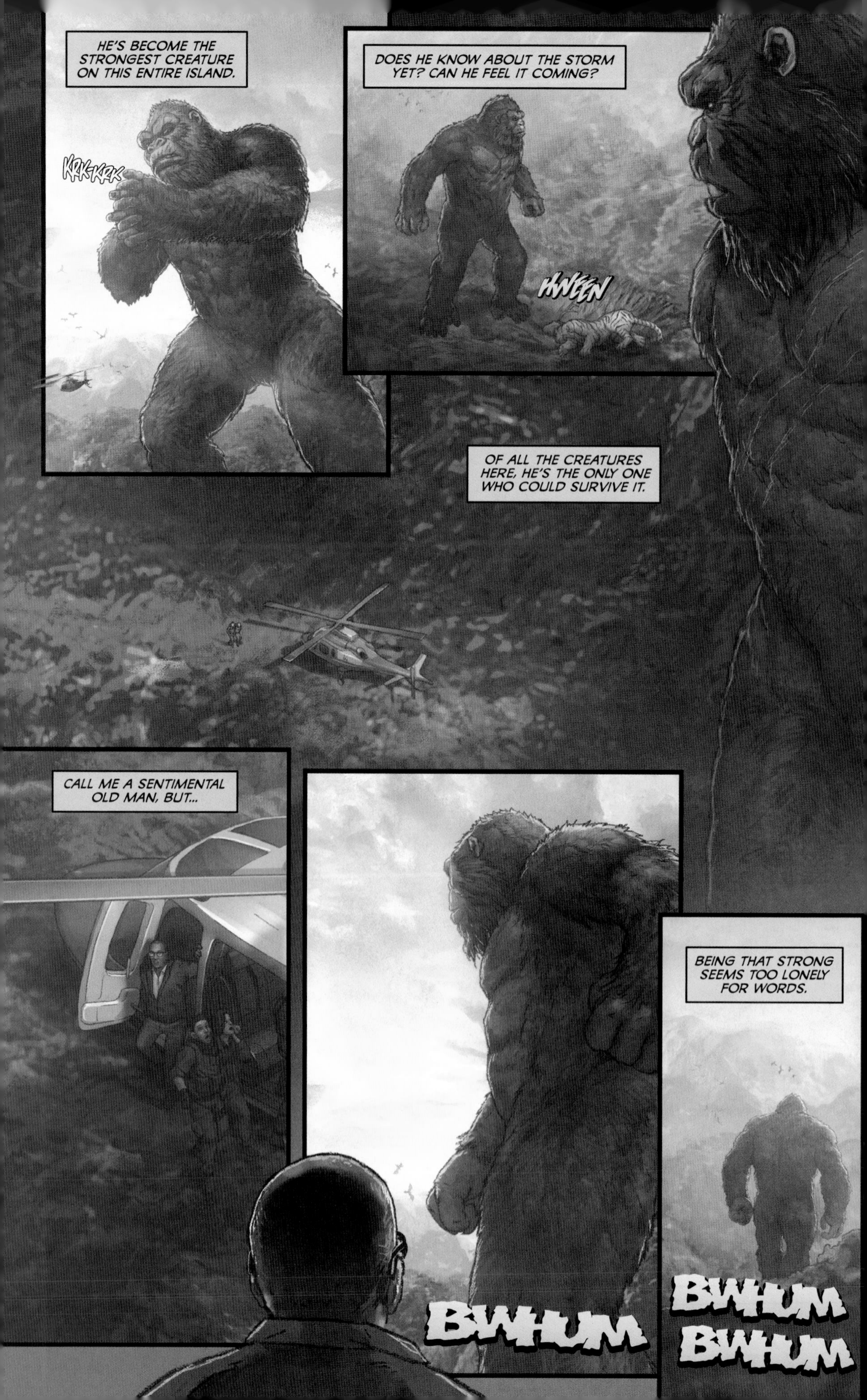
HE'S BECOME THE STRONGEST CREATURE ON THIS ENTIRE ISLAND.
KRK KRK
DOES HE KNOW ABOUT THE STORM YET? CAN HE FEEL IT COMING?
HWEEN
OF ALL THE CREATURES HERE, HE'S THE ONLY ONE WHO COULD SURVIVE IT.
CALL ME A SENTIMENTAL OLD MAN, BUT...
BWHUM
BEING THAT STRONG SEEMS TOO LONELY FOR WORDS.
BWHUM
BWHUM

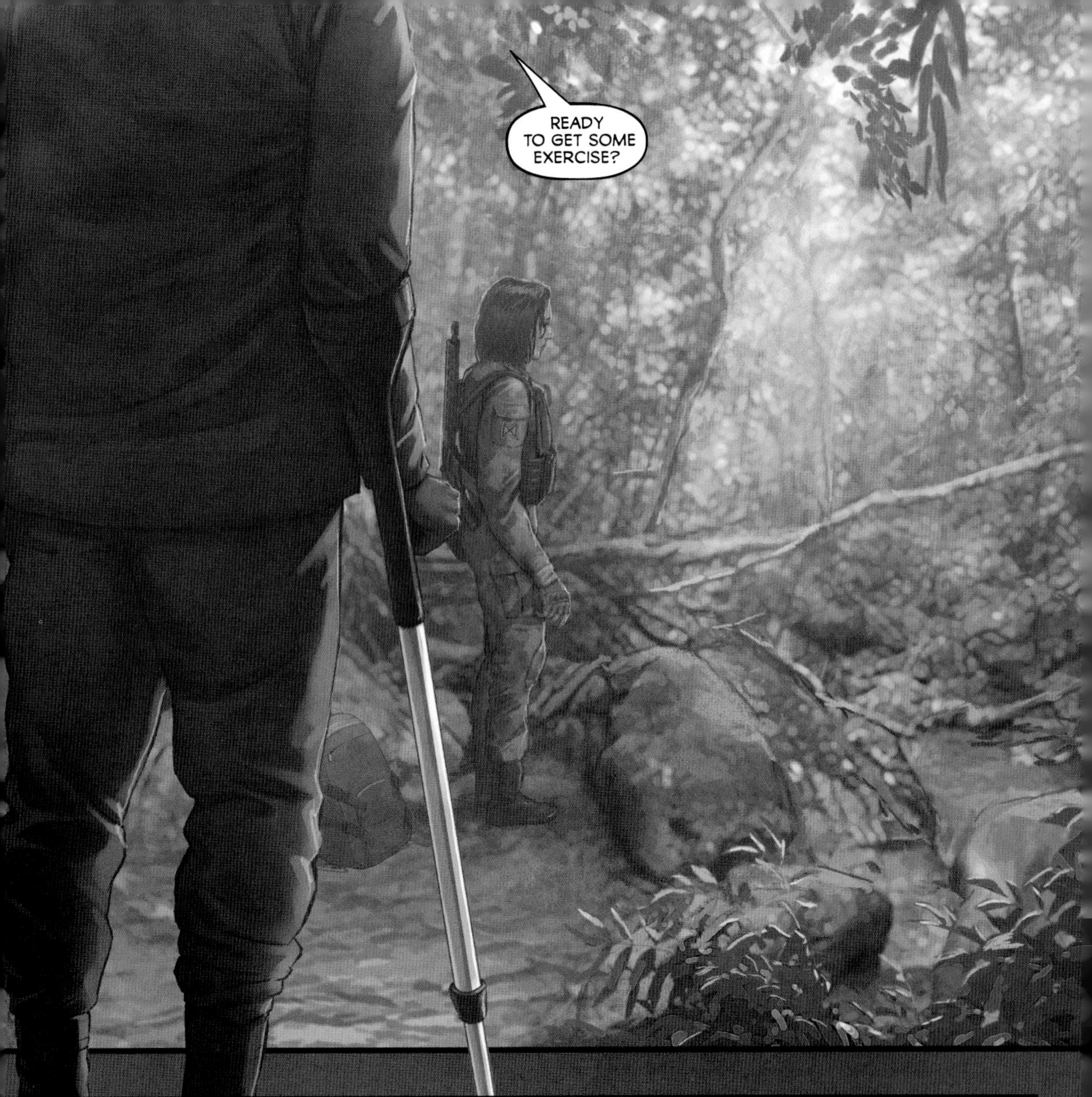
READY TO GET SOME EXERCISE?

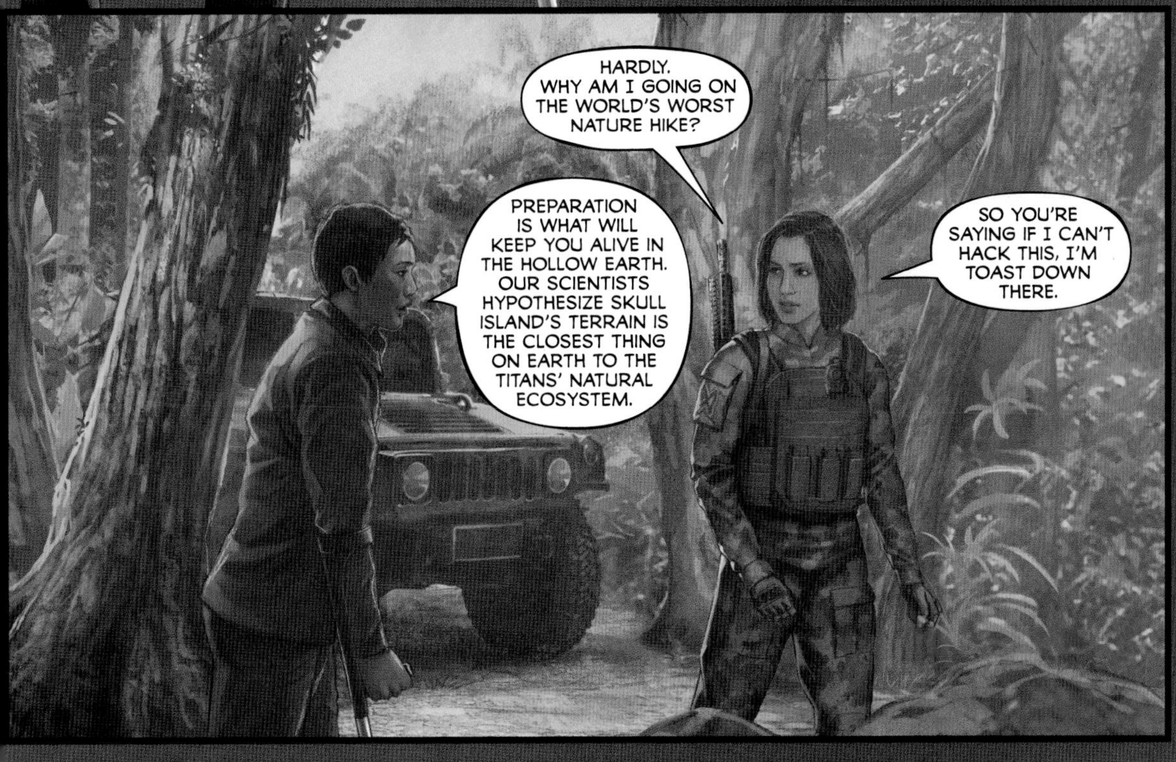
HARDLY. WHY AM I GOING ON THE WORLD'S WORST NATURE HIKE?
PREPARATION IS WHAT WILL KEEP YOU ALIVE IN THE HOLLOW EARTH. OUR SCIENTISTS HYPOTHESIZE SKULL ISLAND'S TERRAIN IS THE CLOSEST THING ON EARTH TO THE TITANS' NATURAL ECOSYSTEM.
SO YOU'RE SAYING IF I CAN'T HACK THIS, I'M TOAST DOWN THERE.

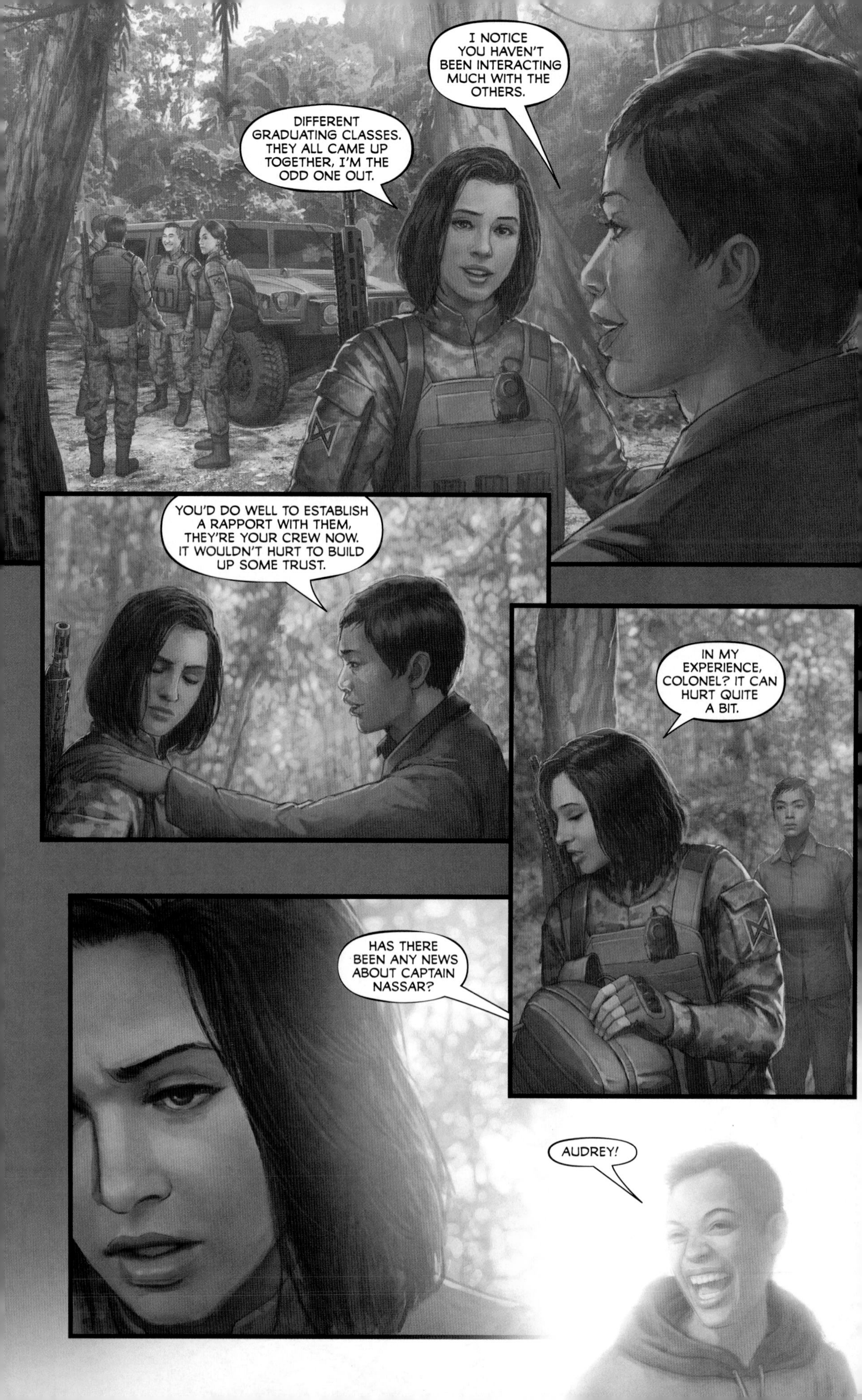
I NOTICE YOU HAVEN'T BEEN INTERACTING MUCH WITH THE OTHERS.
DIFFERENT GRADUATING CLASSES. THEY ALL CAME UP TOGETHER, I'M THE ODD ONE OUT.
YOU'D DO WELL TO ESTABLISH A RAPPORT WITH THEM, THEY'RE YOUR CREW NOW. IT WOULDN'T HURT TO BUILD UP SOME TRUST.
IN MY EXPERIENCE, COLONEL? IT CAN HURT QUITE A BIT.
HAS THERE BEEN ANY NEWS ABOUT CAPTAIN NASSAR?
AUDREY!

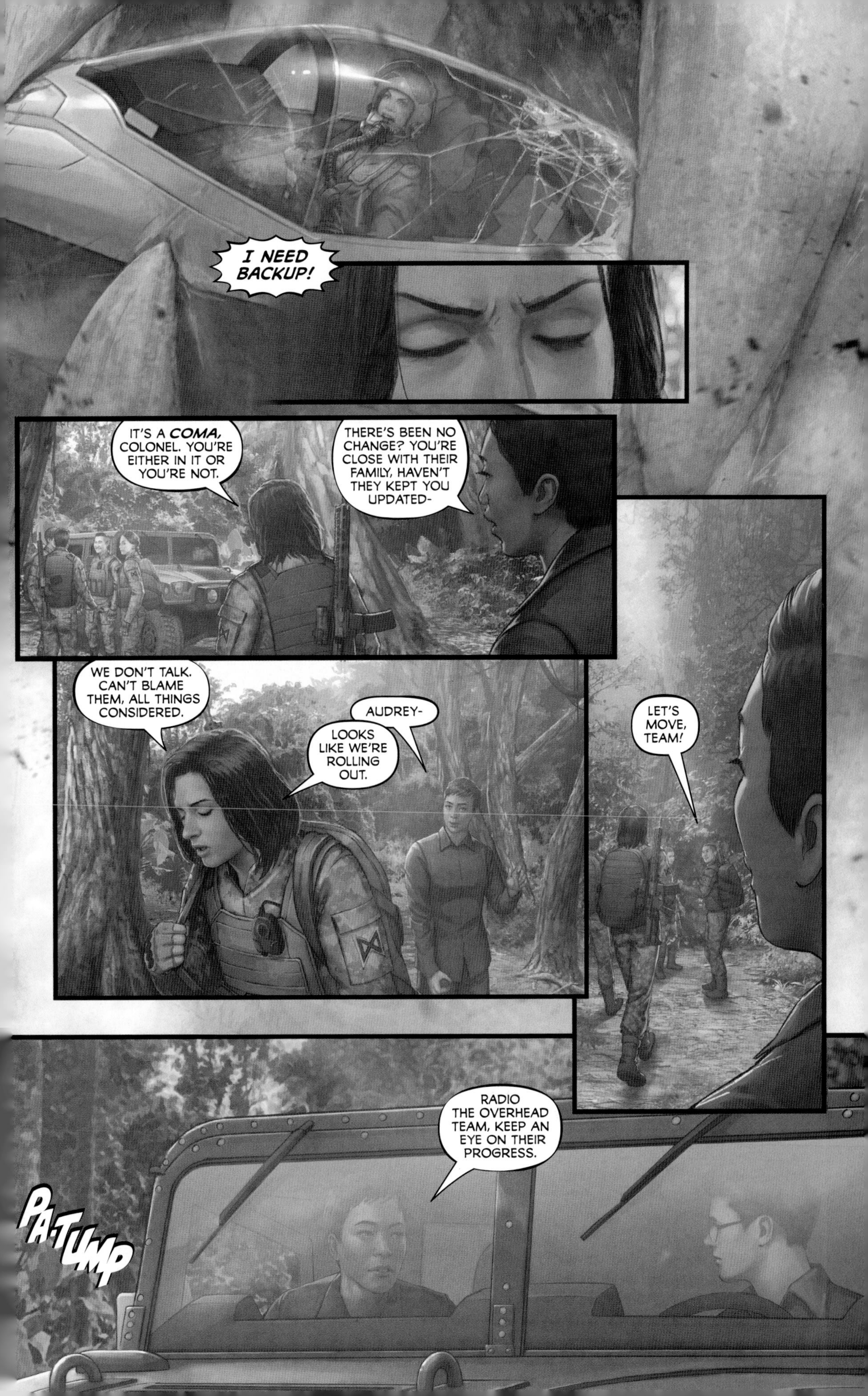
I NEED BACKUP!
IT'S A *COMA,* COLONEL. YOU'RE EITHER IN IT OR YOU'RE NOT.
THERE'S BEEN NO CHANGE? YOU'RE CLOSE WITH THEIR FAMILY, HAVEN'T THEY KEPT YOU UPDATED-
WE DON'T TALK. CAN'T BLAME THEM, ALL THINGS CONSIDERED.
AUDREY-
LOOKS LIKE WE'RE ROLLING OUT.
LET'S MOVE, TEAM!
RADIO THE OVERHEAD TEAM, KEEP AN EYE ON THEIR PROGRESS.
PA-TUMP

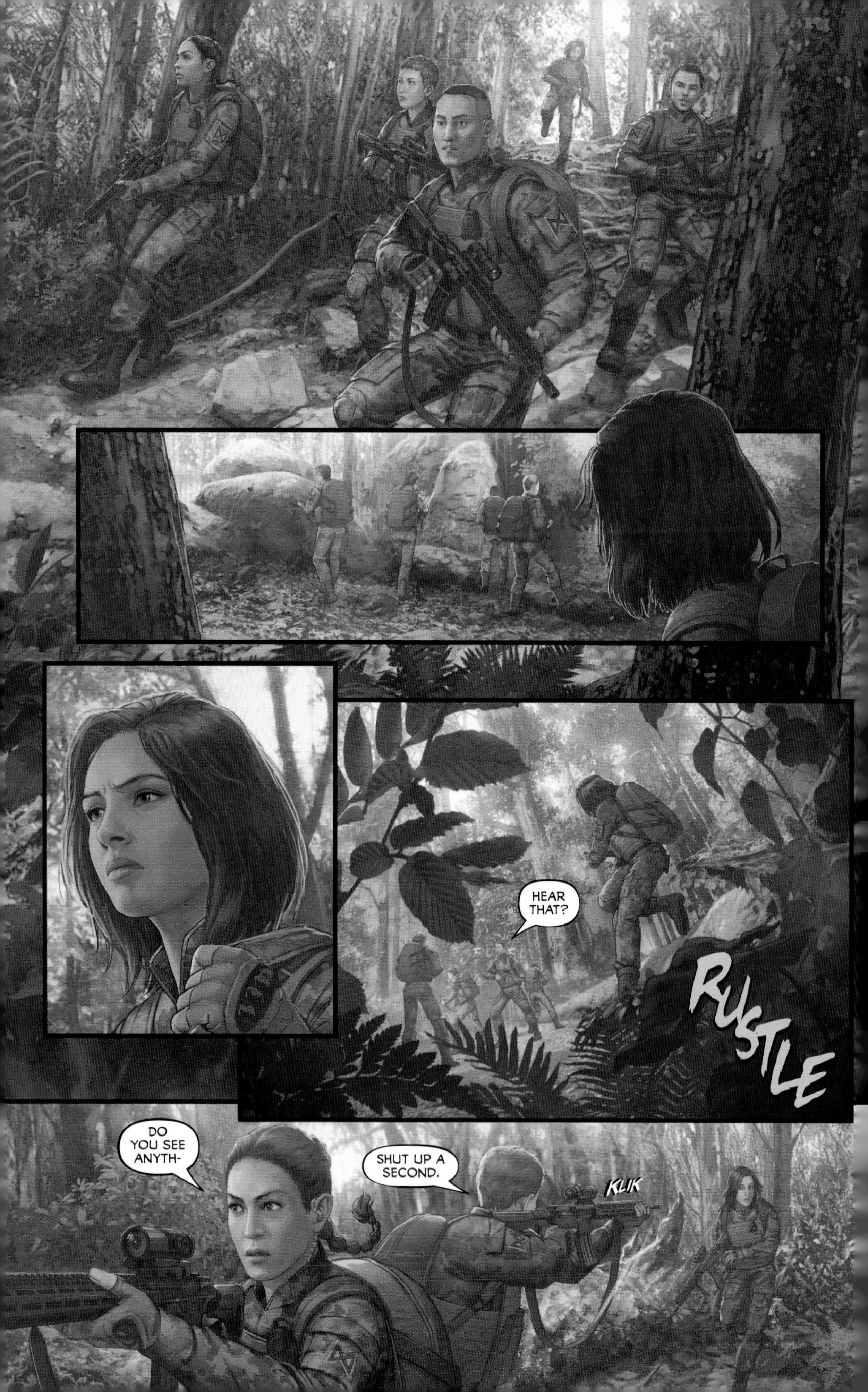
HEAR THAT?
RUSTLE
DO YOU SEE ANYTH-
SHUT UP A SECOND.
KLIK

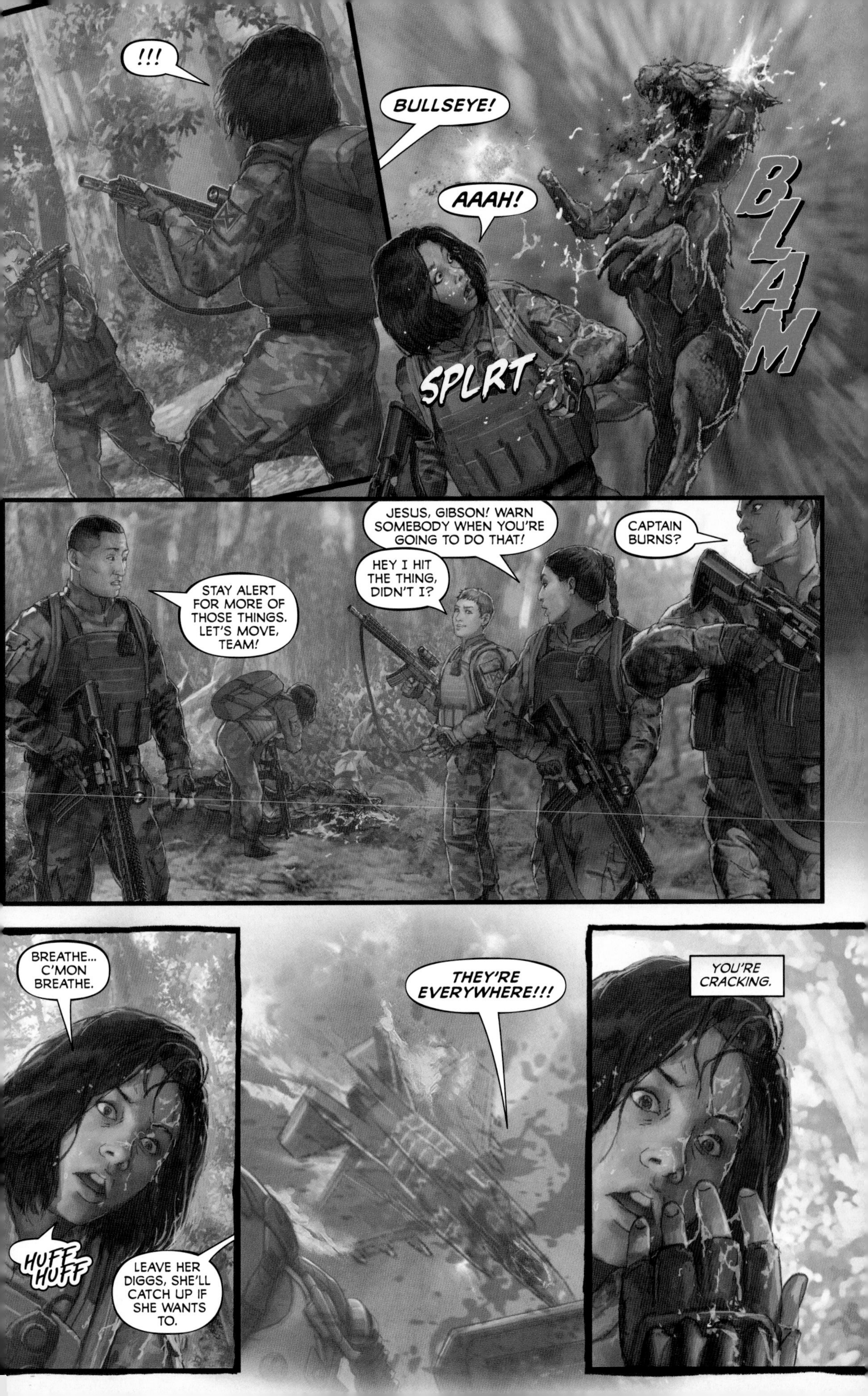
!!!
BULLSEYE!
AAAH!
SPLRT
BLAM
JESUS, GIBSON! WARN SOMEBODY WHEN YOU'RE GOING TO DO THAT!
CAPTAIN BURNS?
HEY I HIT THE THING, DIDN'T I?
STAY ALERT FOR MORE OF THOSE THINGS. LET'S MOVE, TEAM!
BREATHE... C'MON BREATHE.
HUFF HUFF
LEAVE HER DIGGS, SHE'LL CATCH UP IF SHE WANTS TO.
THEY'RE EVERYWHERE!!!
YOU'RE CRACKING.

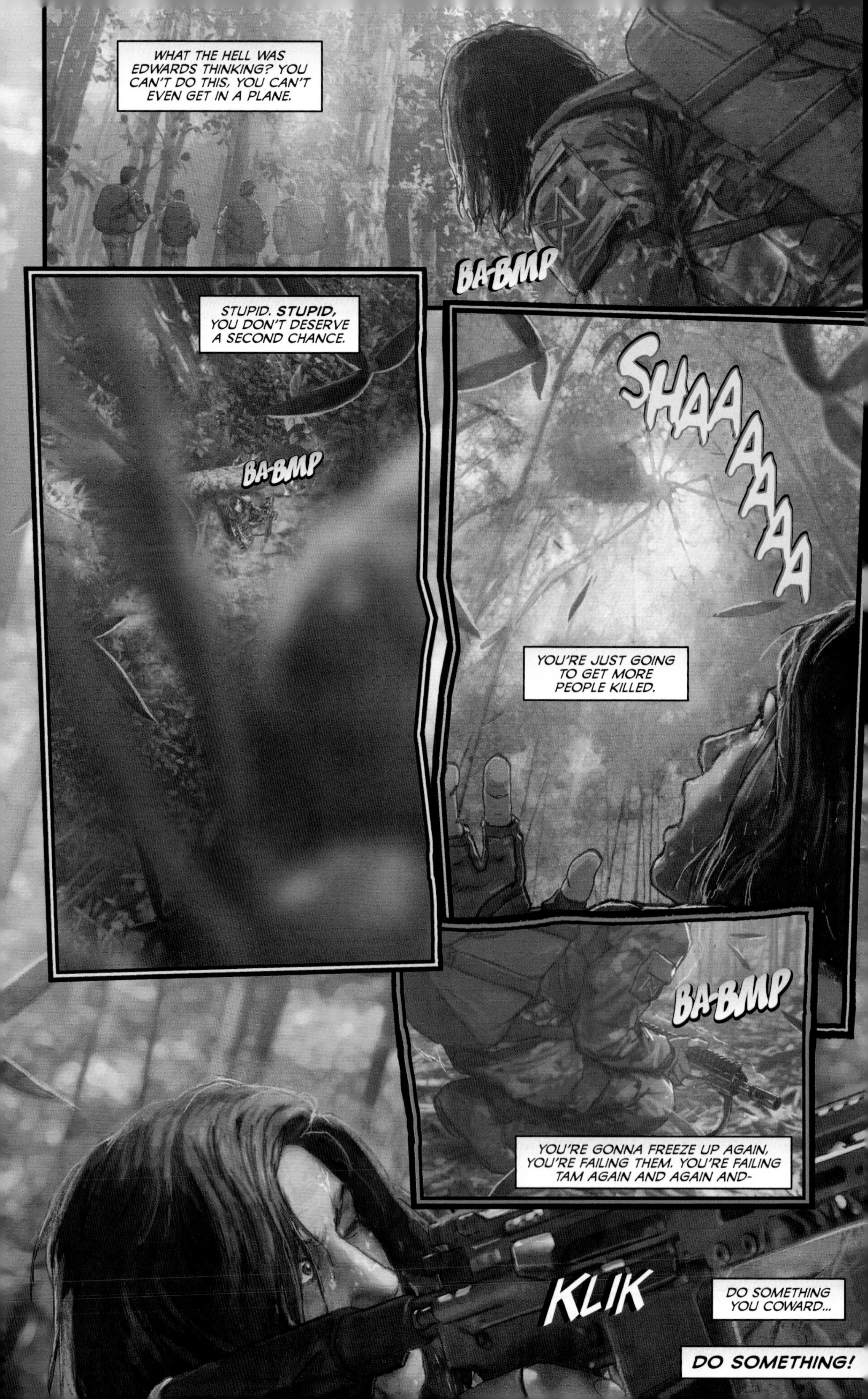

WHAT THE HELL WAS EDWARDS THINKING? YOU CAN'T DO THIS, YOU CAN'T EVEN GET IN A PLANE.
BA-BMP
STUPID. **STUPID,** YOU DON'T DESERVE A SECOND CHANCE.
BA-BMP
SHAAAAAAA
YOU'RE JUST GOING TO GET MORE PEOPLE KILLED.
BA-BMP
YOU'RE GONNA FREEZE UP AGAIN, YOU'RE FAILING THEM. YOU'RE FAILING TAM AGAIN AND AGAIN AND-
KLIK
DO SOMETHING YOU COWARD...
DO SOMETHING!

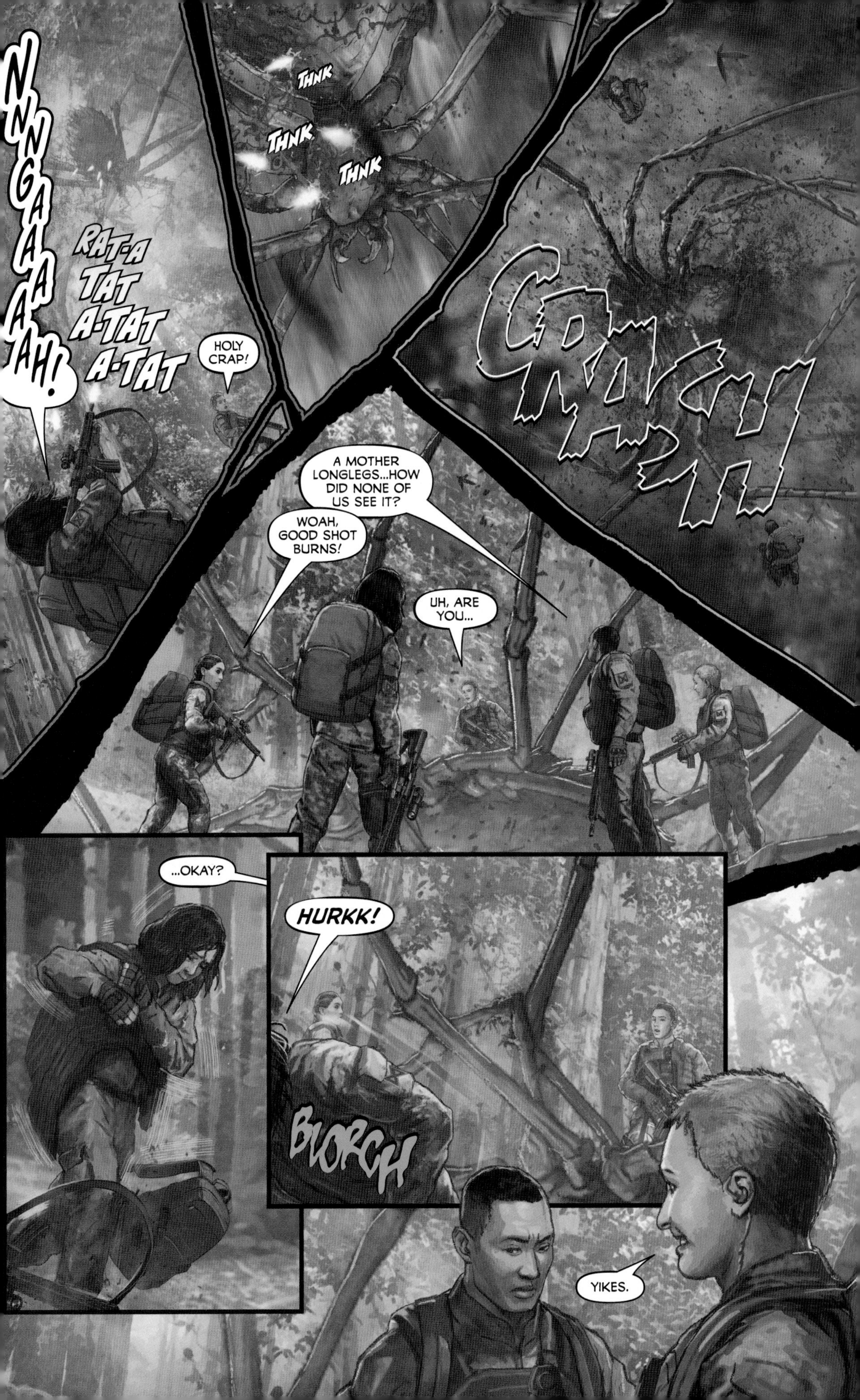
NNNGAAAAAAH!
RAT-A TAT A-TAT A-TAT
HOLY CRAP!
THNK
THNK
THNK
CRACH
A MOTHER LONGLEGS...HOW DID NONE OF US SEE IT?
WOAH, GOOD SHOT BURNS!
UH, ARE YOU...
...OKAY?
HURKK!
BLORCH
YIKES.

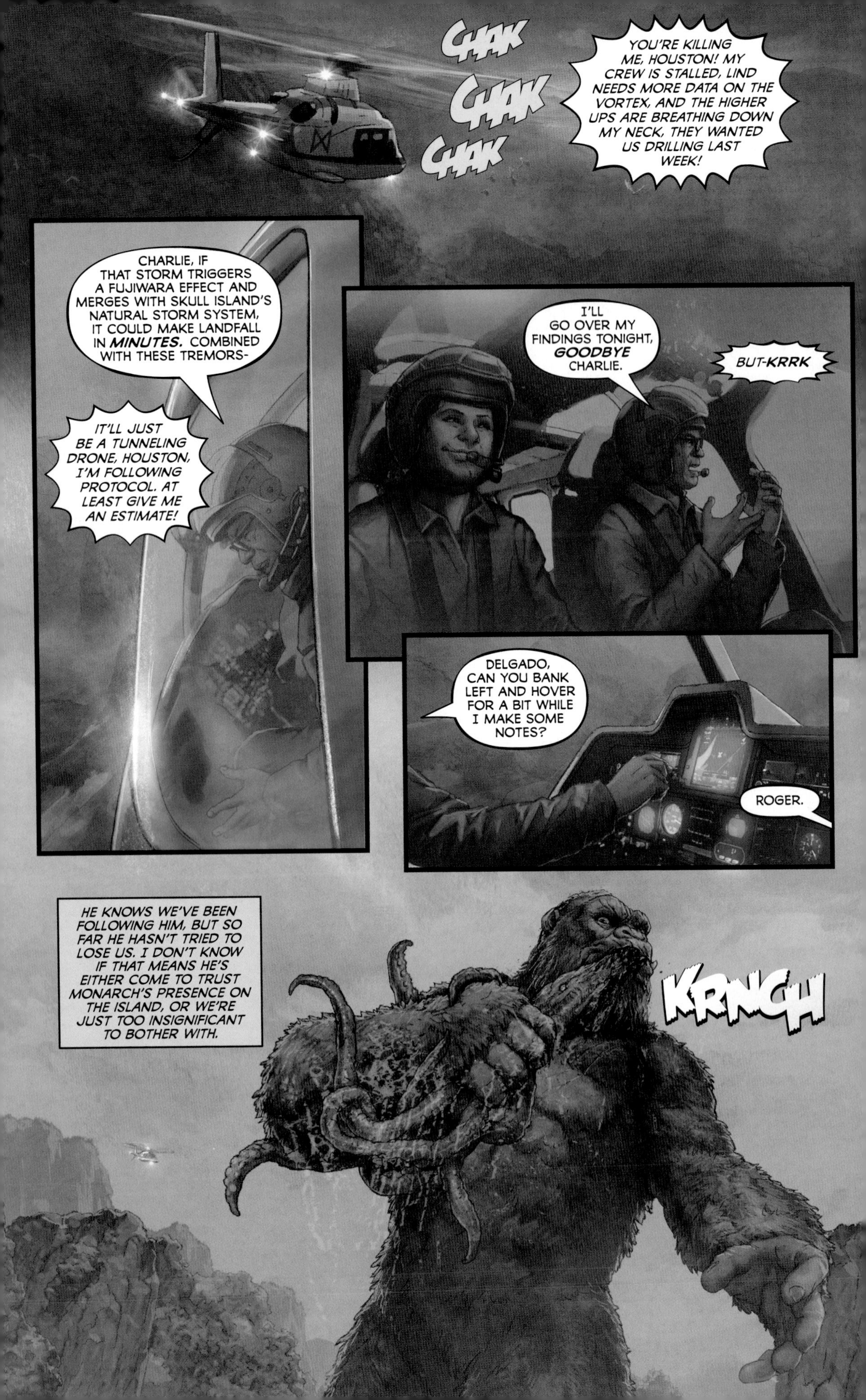
CHAK CHAK CHAK
YOU'RE KILLING ME, HOUSTON! MY CREW IS STALLED, LIND NEEDS MORE DATA ON THE VORTEX, AND THE HIGHER UPS ARE BREATHING DOWN MY NECK, THEY WANTED US DRILLING LAST WEEK!
CHARLIE, IF THAT STORM TRIGGERS A FUJIWARA EFFECT AND MERGES WITH SKULL ISLAND'S NATURAL STORM SYSTEM, IT COULD MAKE LANDFALL IN MINUTES. COMBINED WITH THESE TREMORS-
IT'LL JUST BE A TUNNELING DRONE, HOUSTON, I'M FOLLOWING PROTOCOL. AT LEAST GIVE ME AN ESTIMATE!
I'LL GO OVER MY FINDINGS TONIGHT, GOODBYE CHARLIE.
BUT-KRRK
DELGADO, CAN YOU BANK LEFT AND HOVER FOR A BIT WHILE I MAKE SOME NOTES?
ROGER.
HE KNOWS WE'VE BEEN FOLLOWING HIM, BUT SO FAR HE HASN'T TRIED TO LOSE US. I DON'T KNOW IF THAT MEANS HE'S EITHER COME TO TRUST MONARCH'S PRESENCE ON THE ISLAND, OR WE'RE JUST TOO INSIGNIFICANT TO BOTHER WITH.
KRNCH

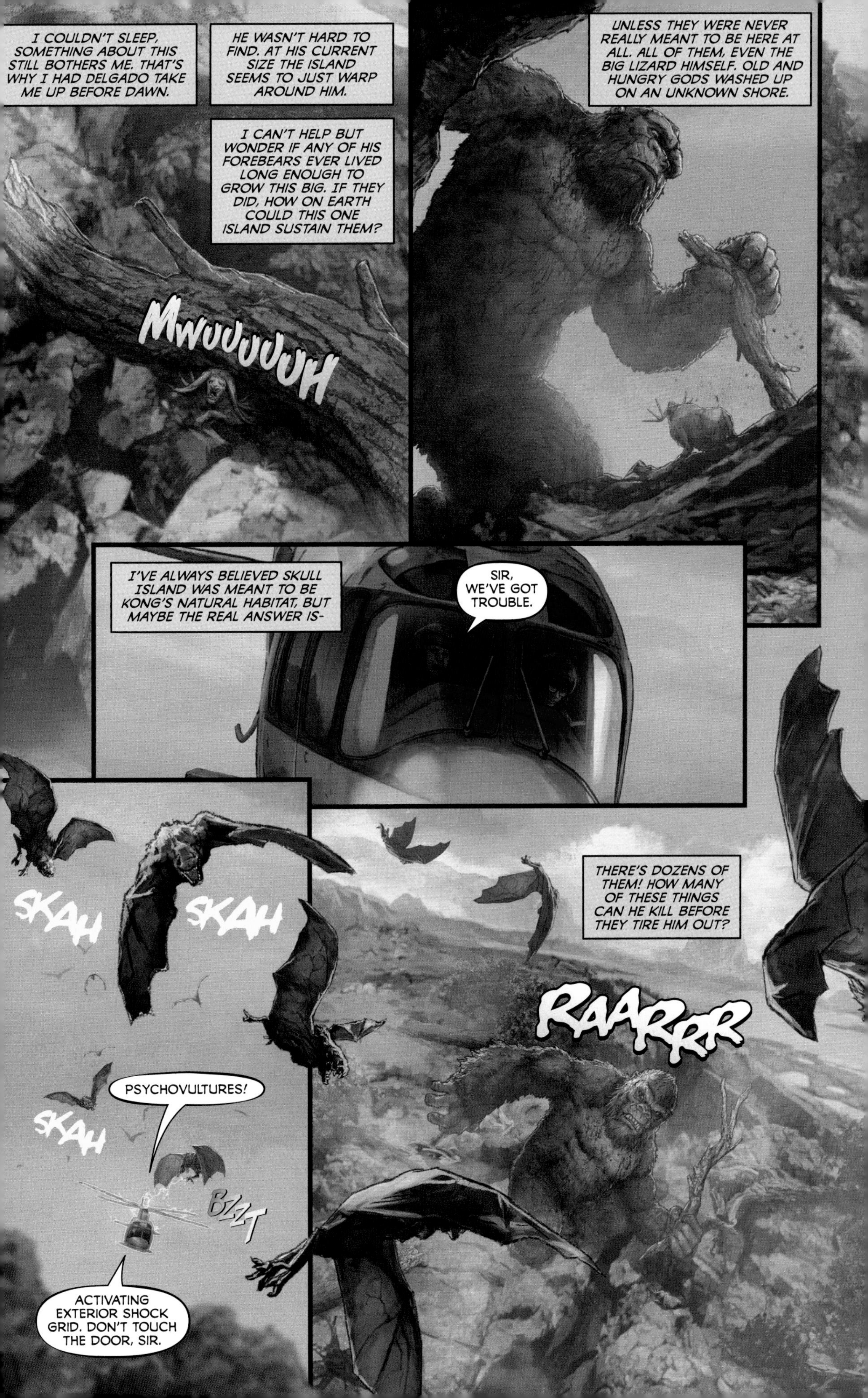
I COULDN'T SLEEP, SOMETHING ABOUT THIS STILL BOTHERS ME. THAT'S WHY I HAD DELGADO TAKE ME UP BEFORE DAWN.
HE WASN'T HARD TO FIND. AT HIS CURRENT SIZE THE ISLAND SEEMS TO JUST WARP AROUND HIM.
I CAN'T HELP BUT WONDER IF ANY OF HIS FOREBEARS EVER LIVED LONG ENOUGH TO GROW THIS BIG. IF THEY DID, HOW ON EARTH COULD THIS ONE ISLAND SUSTAIN THEM?
MWUUUUUUH
UNLESS THEY WERE NEVER REALLY MEANT TO BE HERE AT ALL. ALL OF THEM, EVEN THE BIG LIZARD HIMSELF. OLD AND HUNGRY GODS WASHED UP ON AN UNKNOWN SHORE.
I'VE ALWAYS BELIEVED SKULL ISLAND WAS MEANT TO BE KONG'S NATURAL HABITAT, BUT MAYBE THE REAL ANSWER IS-
SIR, WE'VE GOT TROUBLE.
SKAH
SKAH
PSYCHOVULTURES!
SKAH
BZZT
ACTIVATING EXTERIOR SHOCK GRID. DON'T TOUCH THE DOOR, SIR.
THERE'S DOZENS OF THEM! HOW MANY OF THESE THINGS CAN HE KILL BEFORE THEY TIRE HIM OUT?
RAARRR

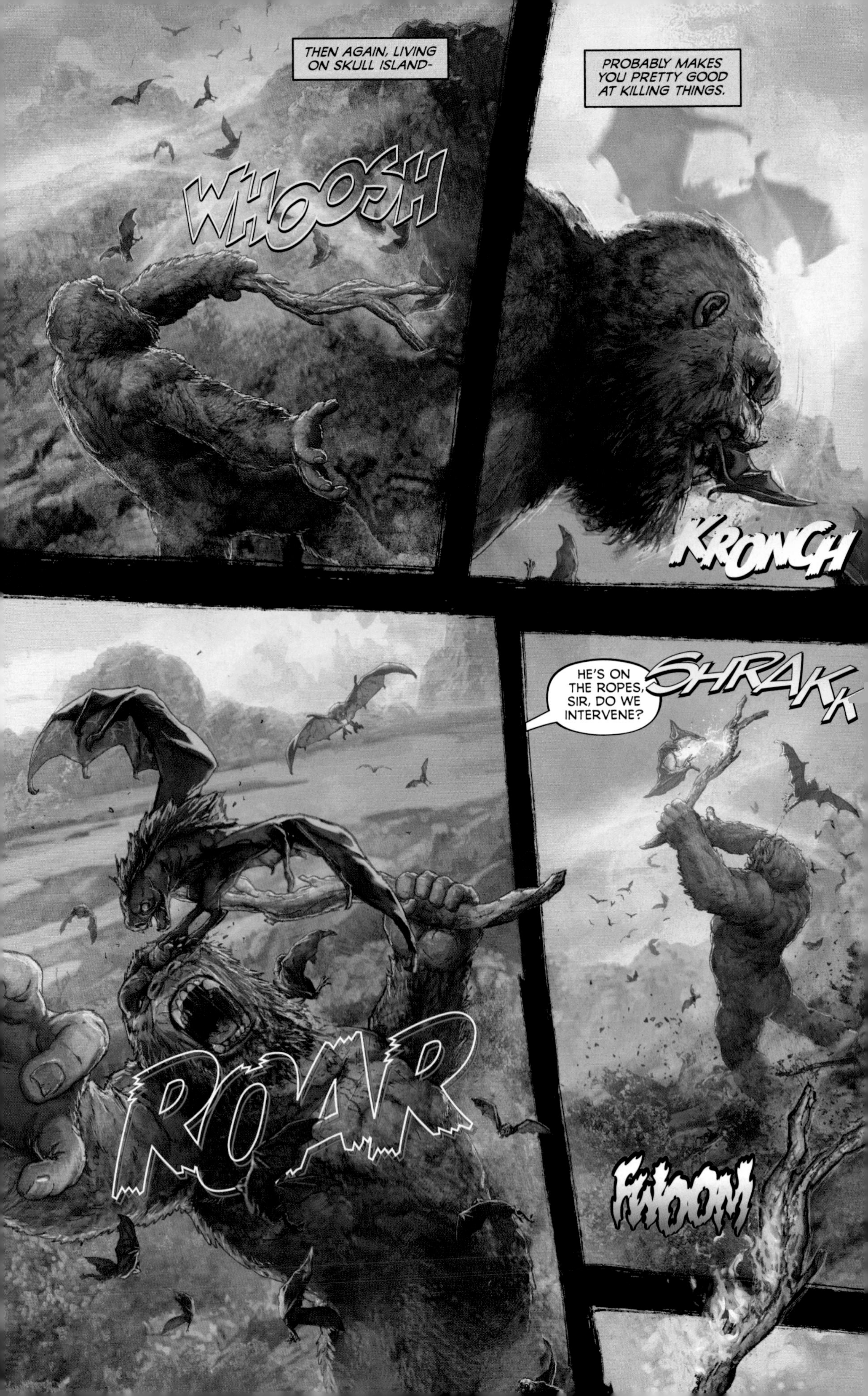
THEN AGAIN, LIVING ON SKULL ISLAND-
WHOOSH
PROBABLY MAKES YOU PRETTY GOOD AT KILLING THINGS.
KRONCH
ROAR
HE'S ON THE ROPES, SIR, DO WE INTERVENE?
SHRAKK
FWOOM

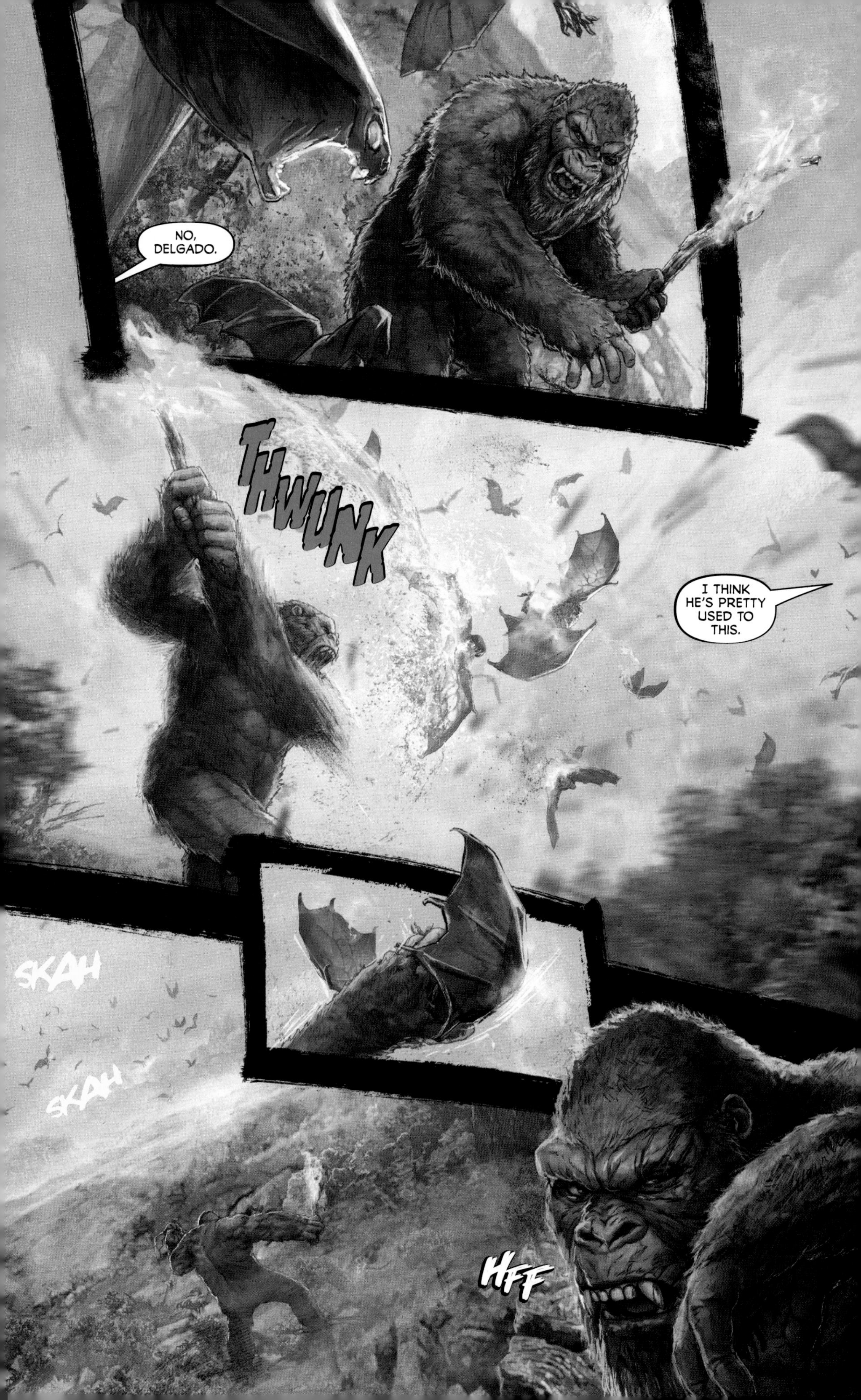
NO, DELGADO.
THWUNK
I THINK HE'S PRETTY USED TO THIS.
SKAH
SKAH
HFF

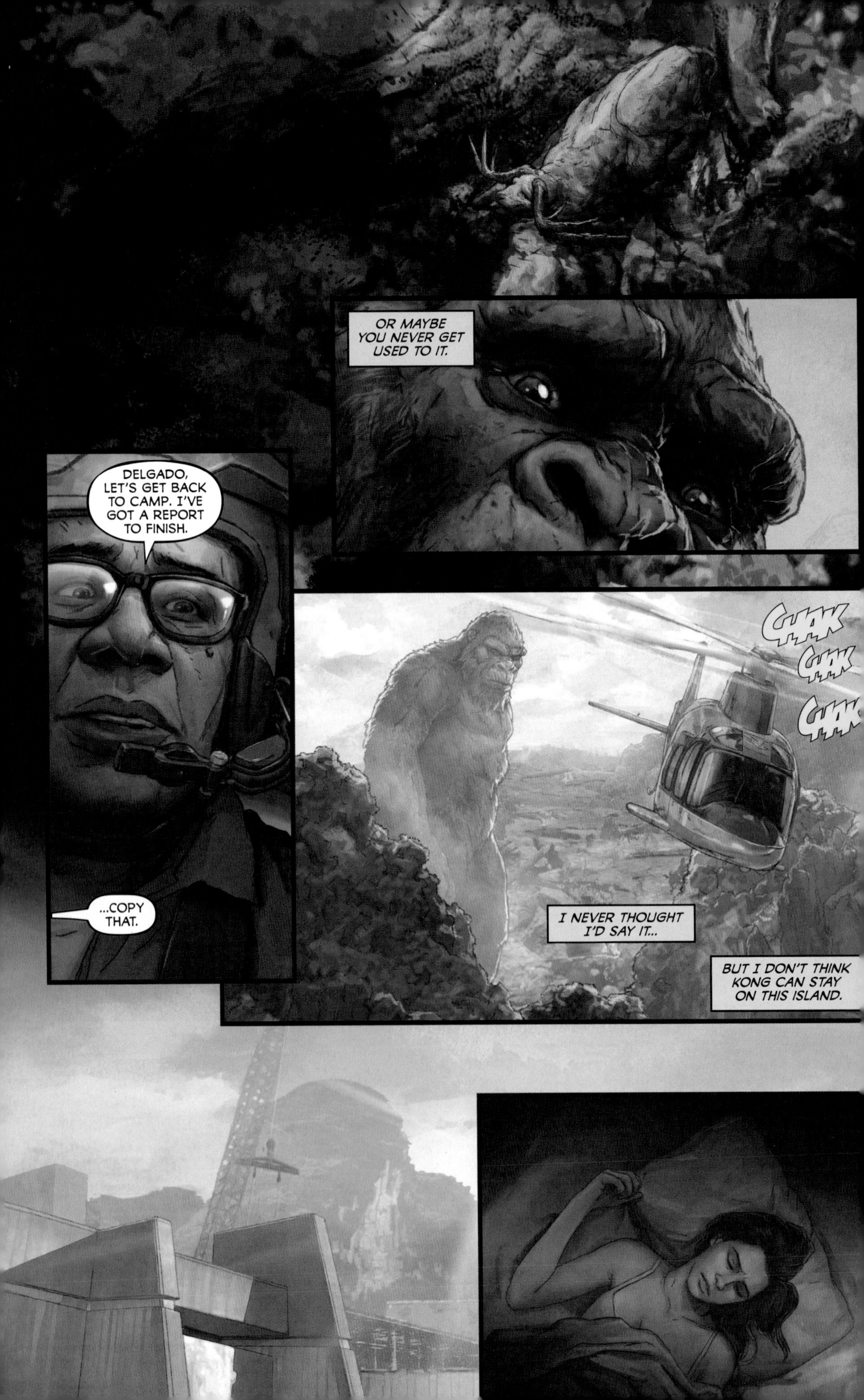
OR MAYBE YOU NEVER GET USED TO IT.
DELGADO, LET'S GET BACK TO CAMP. I'VE GOT A REPORT TO FINISH.
...COPY THAT.
CHAK
CHAK
CHAK
I NEVER THOUGHT I'D SAY IT...
BUT I DON'T THINK KONG CAN STAY ON THIS ISLAND.

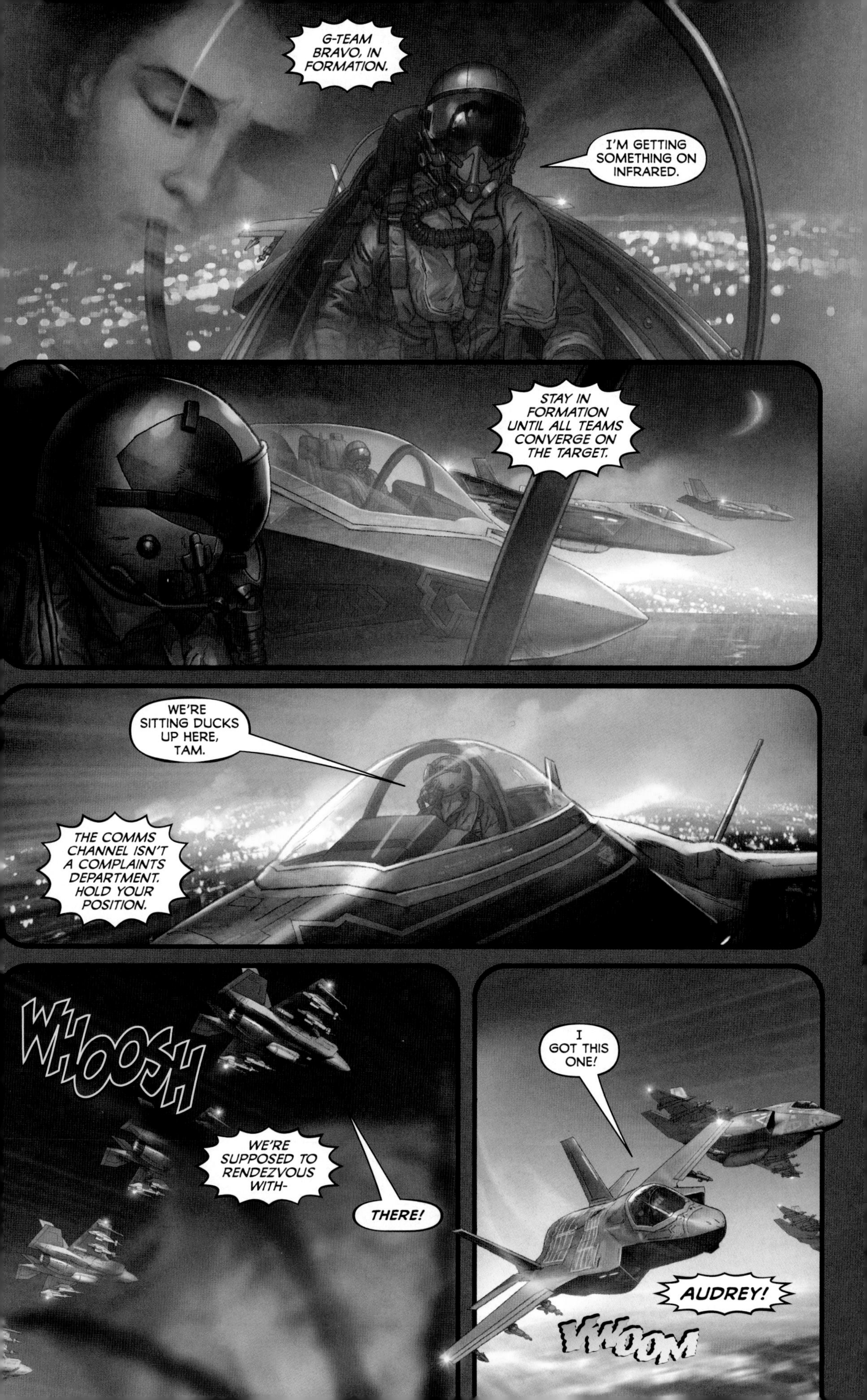
G-TEAM BRAVO, IN FORMATION.
I'M GETTING SOMETHING ON INFRARED.
STAY IN FORMATION UNTIL ALL TEAMS CONVERGE ON THE TARGET.
WE'RE SITTING DUCKS UP HERE, TAM.
THE COMMS CHANNEL ISN'T A COMPLAINTS DEPARTMENT. HOLD YOUR POSITION.
WHOOSH
WE'RE SUPPOSED TO RENDEZVOUS WITH-
THERE!
I GOT THIS ONE!
AUDREY!
VVOOM

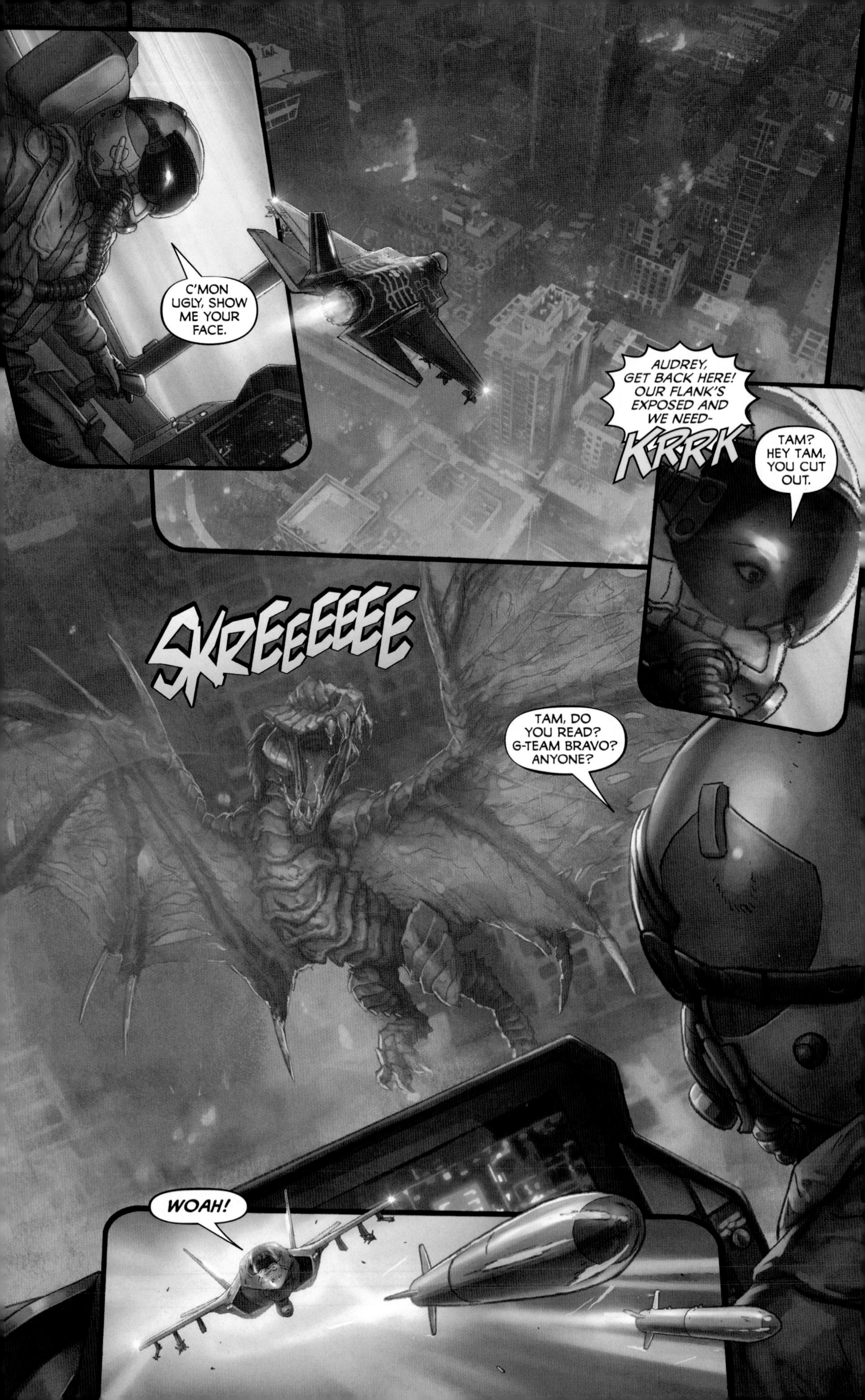
C'MON UGLY, SHOW ME YOUR FACE.
AUDREY, GET BACK HERE! OUR FLANK'S EXPOSED AND WE NEED-
KRRK
TAM? HEY TAM, YOU CUT OUT.
SKREEEEEEE
TAM, DO YOU READ? G-TEAM BRAVO? ANYONE?
WOAH!

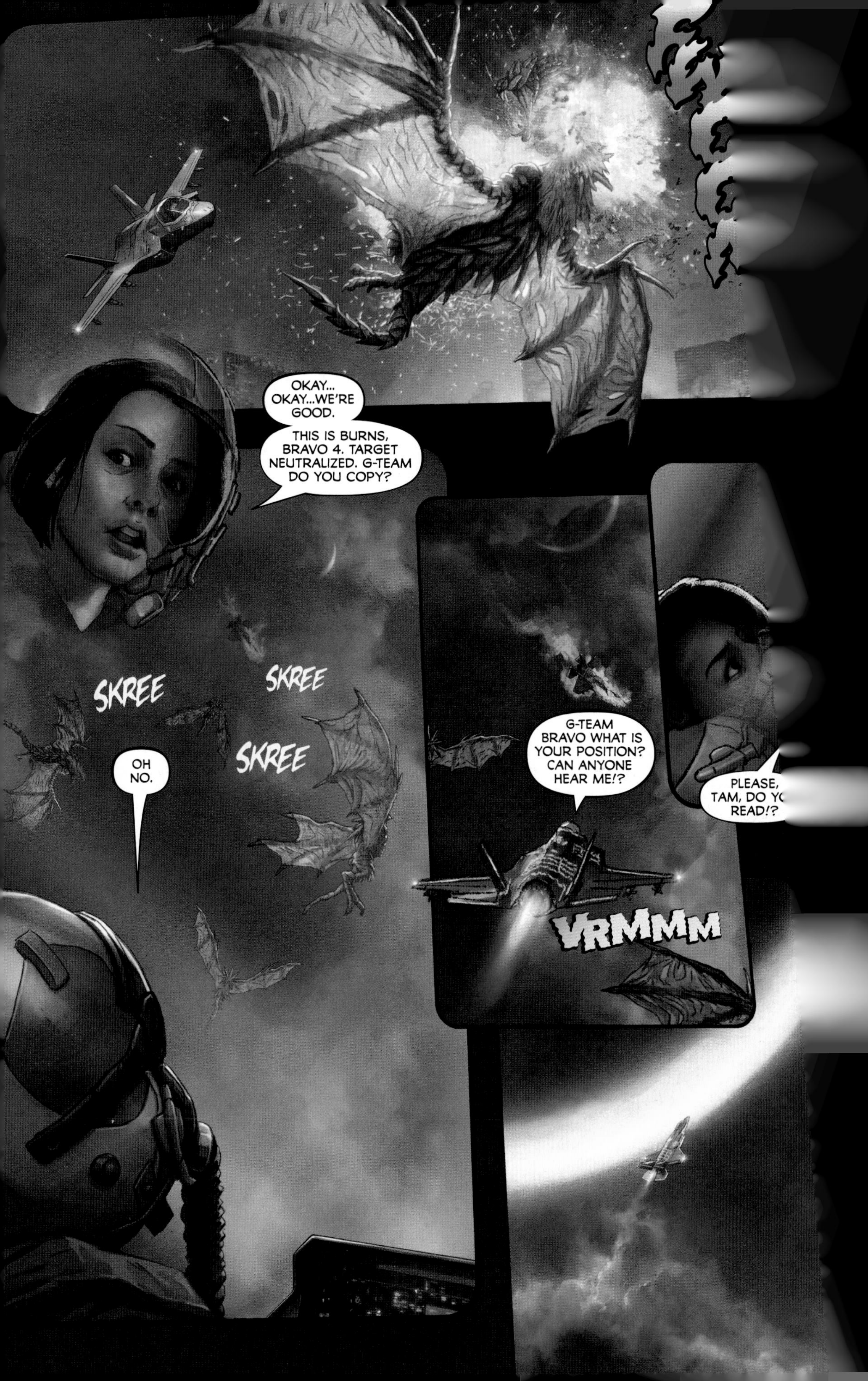
OKAY... OKAY...WE'RE GOOD.
THIS IS BURNS, BRAVO 4. TARGET NEUTRALIZED. G-TEAM DO YOU COPY?
SKREE
SKREE
SKREE
OH NO.
G-TEAM BRAVO WHAT IS YOUR POSITION? CAN ANYONE HEAR ME!?
PLEASE, TAM, DO YO
READ!?
VRMMMM

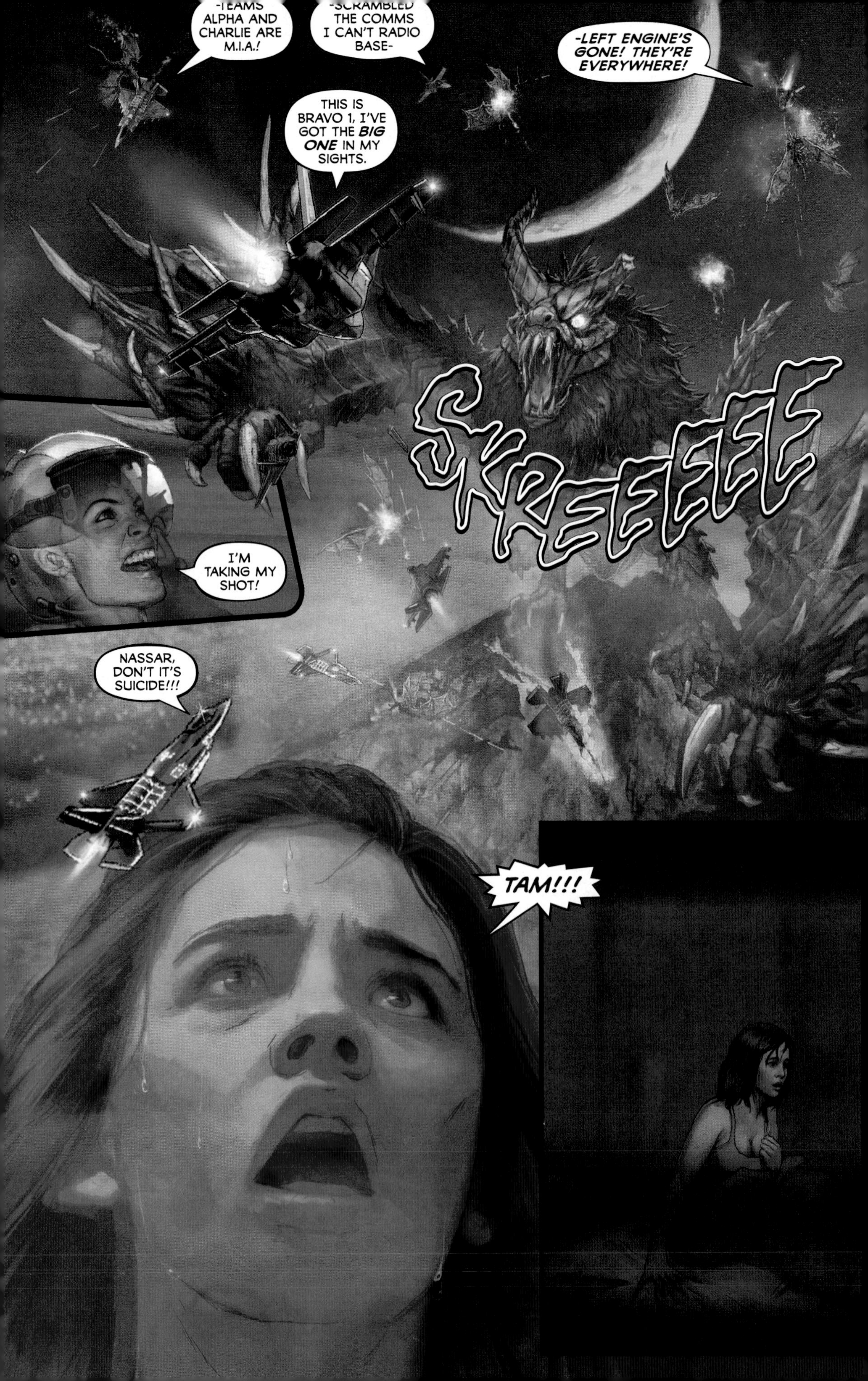
-TEAMS ALPHA AND CHARLIE ARE M.I.A.!
-SCRAMBLED THE COMMS I CAN'T RADIO BASE-
-LEFT ENGINE'S GONE! THEY'RE EVERYWHERE!
THIS IS BRAVO 1, I'VE GOT THE *BIG ONE* IN MY SIGHTS.
SKREEEEEE
I'M TAKING MY SHOT!
NASSAR, DON'T IT'S SUICIDE!!!
TAM!!!

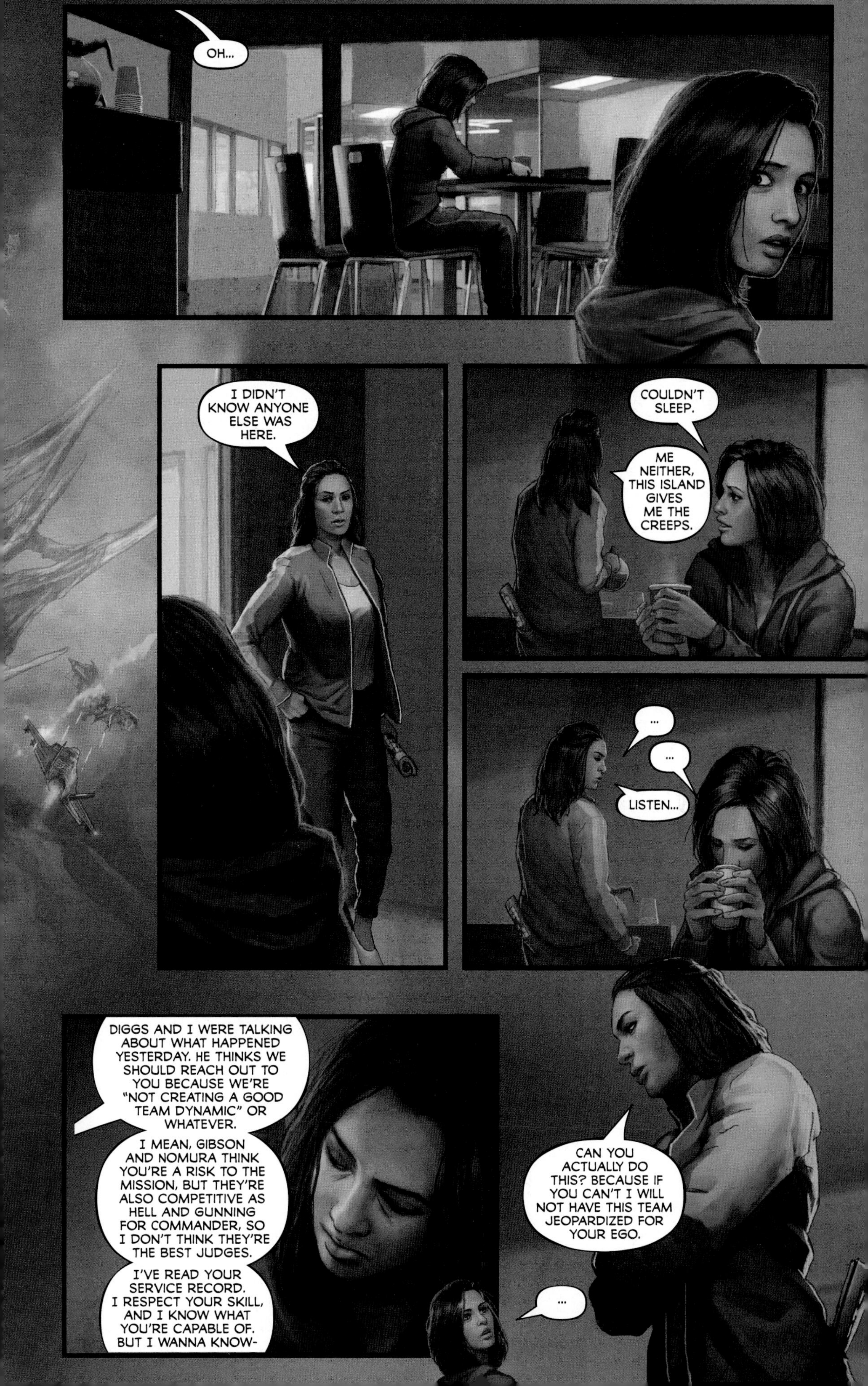
OH...
I DIDN'T KNOW ANYONE ELSE WAS HERE.
COULDN'T SLEEP.
ME NEITHER, THIS ISLAND GIVES ME THE CREEPS.
...
...
LISTEN...
DIGGS AND I WERE TALKING ABOUT WHAT HAPPENED YESTERDAY. HE THINKS WE SHOULD REACH OUT TO YOU BECAUSE WE'RE "NOT CREATING A GOOD TEAM DYNAMIC" OR WHATEVER.
I MEAN, GIBSON AND NOMURA THINK YOU'RE A RISK TO THE MISSION, BUT THEY'RE ALSO COMPETITIVE AS HELL AND GUNNING FOR COMMANDER, SO I DON'T THINK THEY'RE THE BEST JUDGES.
I'VE READ YOUR SERVICE RECORD. I RESPECT YOUR SKILL, AND I KNOW WHAT YOU'RE CAPABLE OF. BUT I WANNA KNOW-
CAN YOU ACTUALLY DO THIS? BECAUSE IF YOU CAN'T I WILL NOT HAVE THIS TEAM JEOPARDIZED FOR YOUR EGO.
...

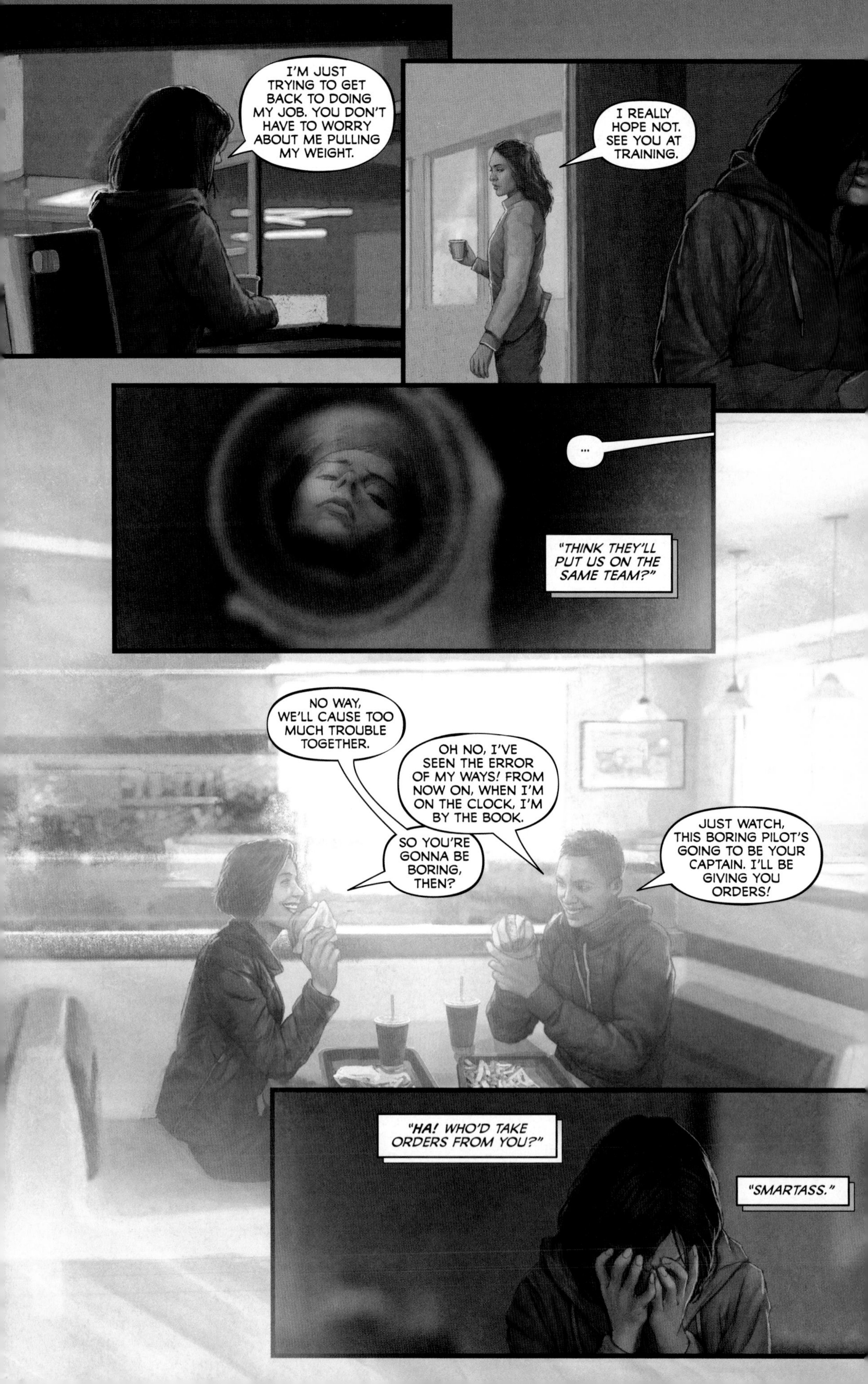
I'M JUST TRYING TO GET BACK TO DOING MY JOB. YOU DON'T HAVE TO WORRY ABOUT ME PULLING MY WEIGHT.
I REALLY HOPE NOT. SEE YOU AT TRAINING.
...
"THINK THEY'LL PUT US ON THE SAME TEAM?"
NO WAY, WE'LL CAUSE TOO MUCH TROUBLE TOGETHER.
OH NO, I'VE SEEN THE ERROR OF MY WAYS! FROM NOW ON, WHEN I'M ON THE CLOCK, I'M BY THE BOOK.
SO YOU'RE GONNA BE BORING, THEN?
JUST WATCH, THIS BORING PILOT'S GOING TO BE YOUR CAPTAIN. I'LL BE GIVING YOU ORDERS!
"HA! WHO'D TAKE ORDERS FROM YOU?"
"SMARTASS."

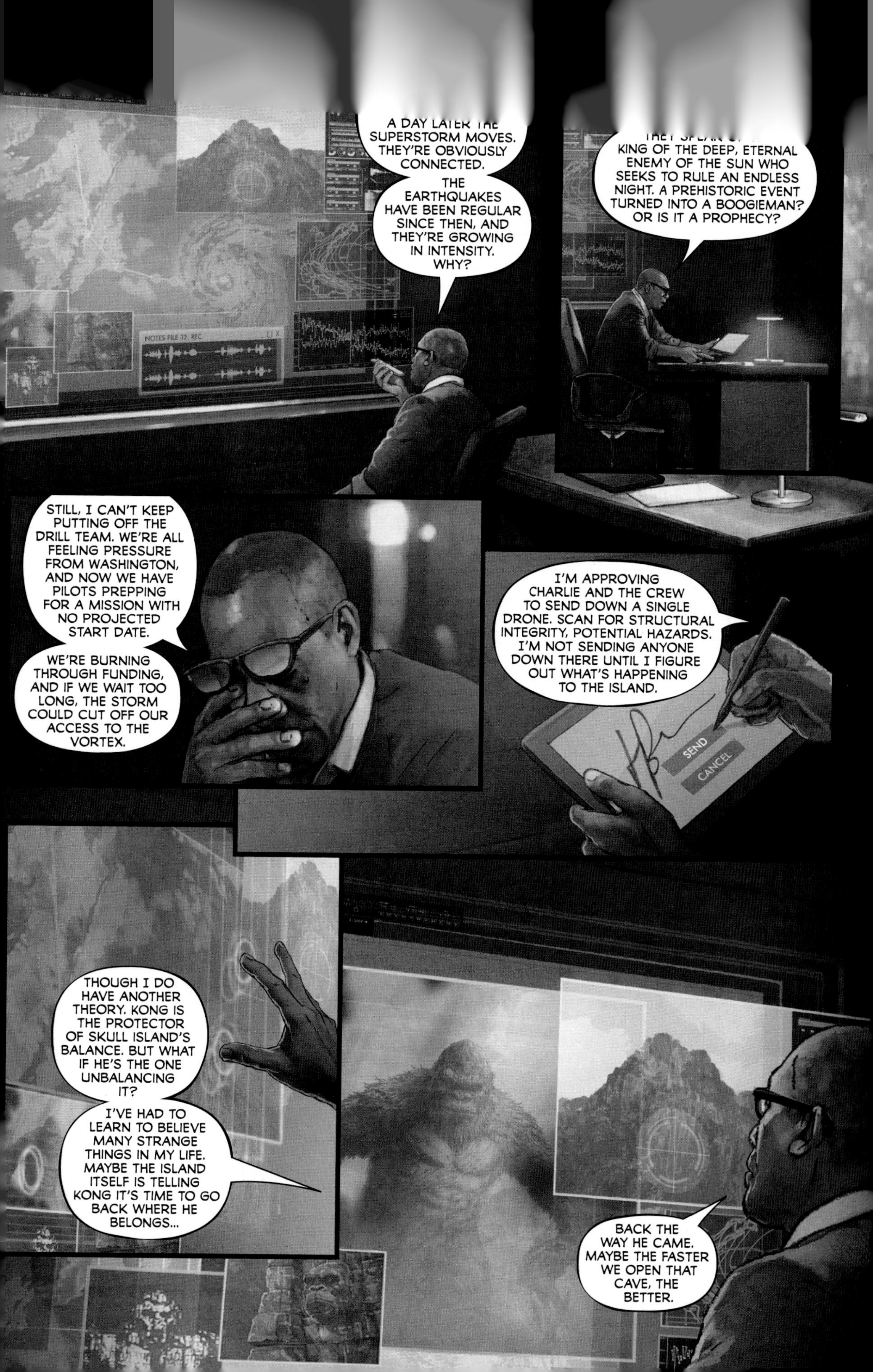
A DAY LATER
SUPERSTORM MOVES. THEY'RE OBVIOUSLY CONNECTED.
THE EARTHQUAKES HAVE BEEN REGULAR SINCE THEN, AND THEY'RE GROWING IN INTENSITY. WHY?
NOTES FILE 32. REC.
KING OF THE DEEP, ETERNAL ENEMY OF THE SUN WHO SEEKS TO RULE AN ENDLESS NIGHT. A PREHISTORIC EVENT TURNED INTO A BOOGIEMAN? OR IS IT A PROPHECY?
STILL, I CAN'T KEEP PUTTING OFF THE DRILL TEAM. WE'RE ALL FEELING PRESSURE FROM WASHINGTON, AND NOW WE HAVE PILOTS PREPPING FOR A MISSION WITH NO PROJECTED START DATE.
WE'RE BURNING THROUGH FUNDING, AND IF WE WAIT TOO LONG, THE STORM COULD CUT OFF OUR ACCESS TO THE VORTEX.
I'M APPROVING CHARLIE AND THE CREW TO SEND DOWN A SINGLE DRONE. SCAN FOR STRUCTURAL INTEGRITY, POTENTIAL HAZARDS. I'M NOT SENDING ANYONE DOWN THERE UNTIL I FIGURE OUT WHAT'S HAPPENING TO THE ISLAND.
SEND
CANCEL
THOUGH I DO HAVE ANOTHER THEORY. KONG IS THE PROTECTOR OF SKULL ISLAND'S BALANCE. BUT WHAT IF HE'S THE ONE UNBALANCING IT?
I'VE HAD TO LEARN TO BELIEVE MANY STRANGE THINGS IN MY LIFE. MAYBE THE ISLAND ITSELF IS TELLING KONG IT'S TIME TO GO BACK WHERE HE BELONGS...
BACK THE WAY HE CAME. MAYBE THE FASTER WE OPEN THAT CAVE, THE BETTER.

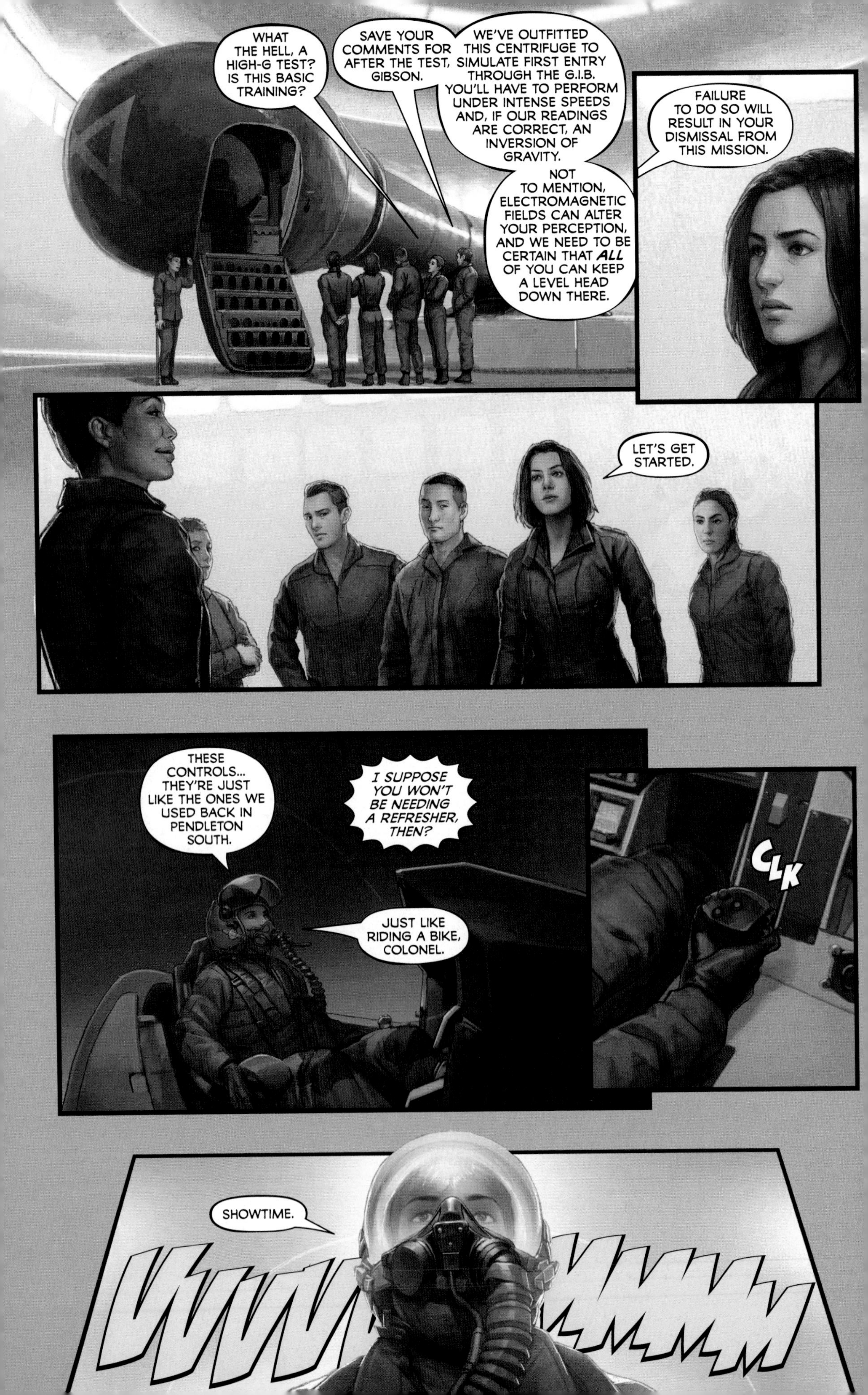
WHAT THE HELL, A HIGH-G TEST? IS THIS BASIC TRAINING?
SAVE YOUR COMMENTS FOR AFTER THE TEST, GIBSON.
WE'VE OUTFITTED THIS CENTRIFUGE TO SIMULATE FIRST ENTRY THROUGH THE G.I.B. YOU'LL HAVE TO PERFORM UNDER INTENSE SPEEDS AND, IF OUR READINGS ARE CORRECT, AN INVERSION OF GRAVITY.
NOT TO MENTION, ELECTROMAGNETIC FIELDS CAN ALTER YOUR PERCEPTION, AND WE NEED TO BE CERTAIN THAT *ALL* OF YOU CAN KEEP A LEVEL HEAD DOWN THERE.
FAILURE TO DO SO WILL RESULT IN YOUR DISMISSAL FROM THIS MISSION.
LET'S GET STARTED.
THESE CONTROLS... THEY'RE JUST LIKE THE ONES WE USED BACK IN PENDLETON SOUTH.
I SUPPOSE YOU WON'T BE NEEDING A REFRESHER, THEN?
JUST LIKE RIDING A BIKE, COLONEL.
CLK
SHOWTIME.
VVVMMMMMM

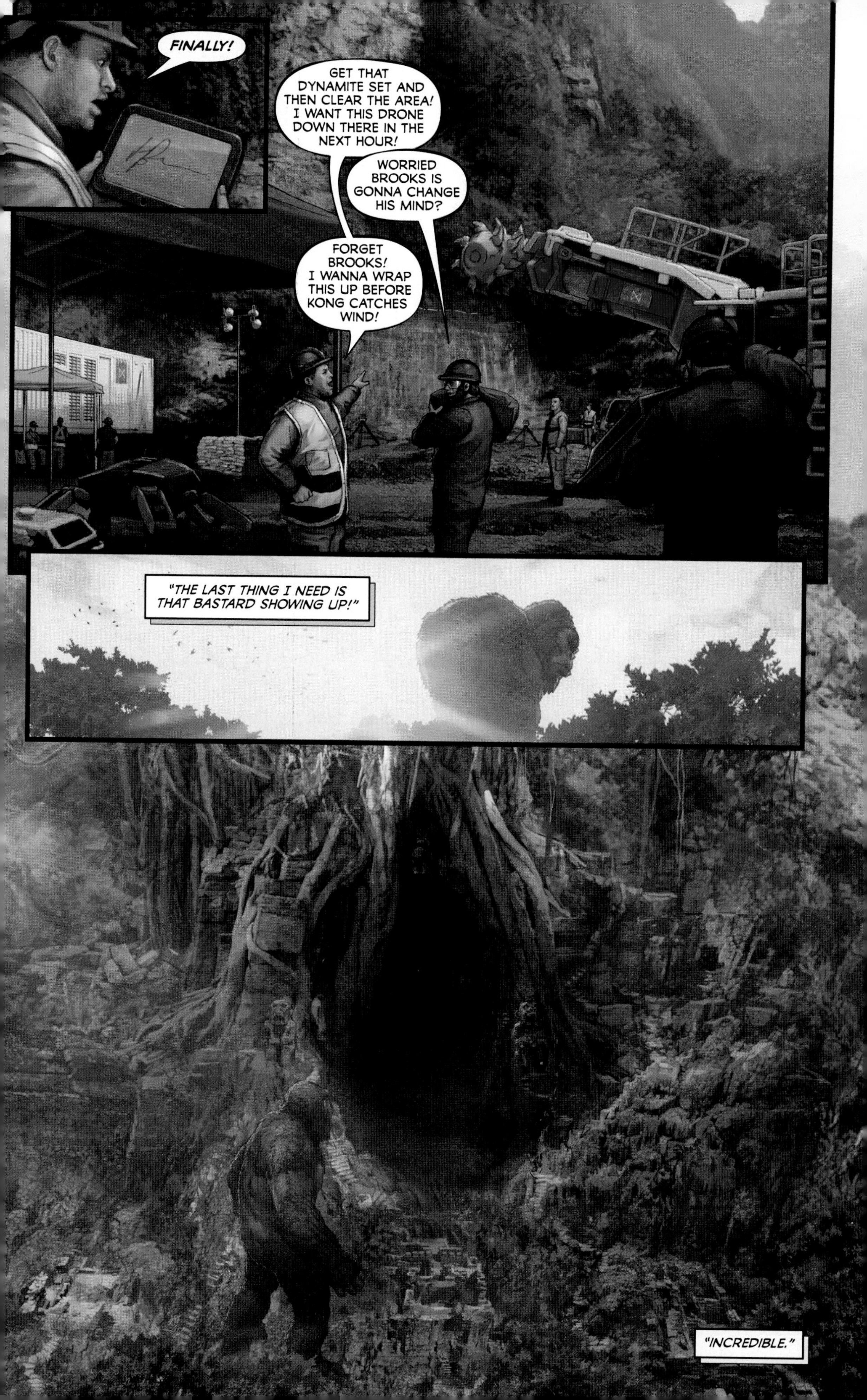
FINALLY!
GET THAT DYNAMITE SET AND THEN CLEAR THE AREA! I WANT THIS DRONE DOWN THERE IN THE NEXT HOUR!
WORRIED BROOKS IS GONNA CHANGE HIS MIND?
FORGET BROOKS! I WANNA WRAP THIS UP BEFORE KONG CATCHES WIND!
"THE LAST THING I NEED IS THAT BASTARD SHOWING UP!"
"INCREDIBLE."

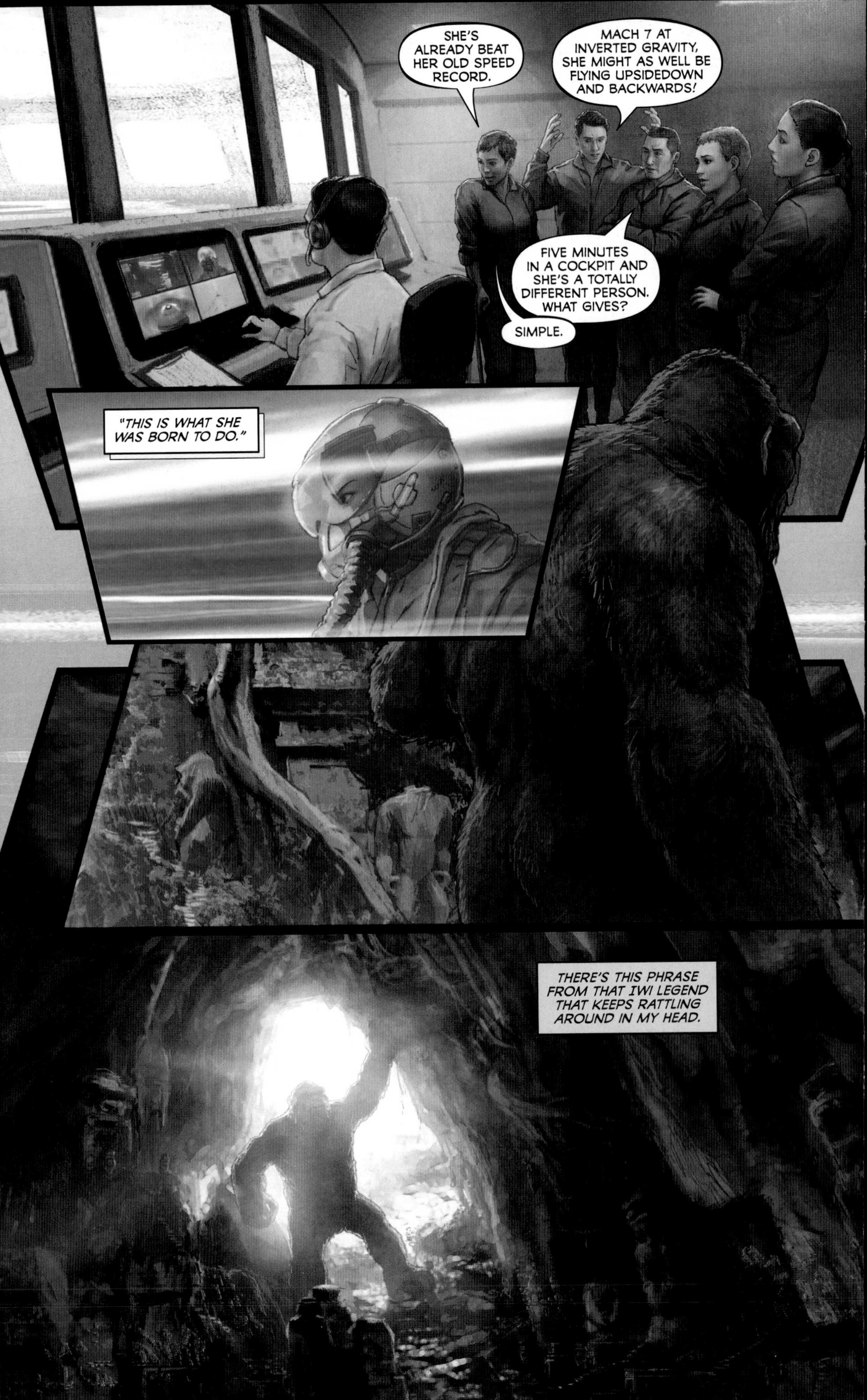
SHE'S ALREADY BEAT HER OLD SPEED RECORD.
MACH 7 AT INVERTED GRAVITY, SHE MIGHT AS WELL BE FLYING UPSIDEDOWN AND BACKWARDS!
FIVE MINUTES IN A COCKPIT AND SHE'S A TOTALLY DIFFERENT PERSON. WHAT GIVES?
SIMPLE.
"THIS IS WHAT SHE WAS BORN TO DO."
THERE'S THIS PHRASE FROM THAT IWI LEGEND THAT KEEPS RATTLING AROUND IN MY HEAD.

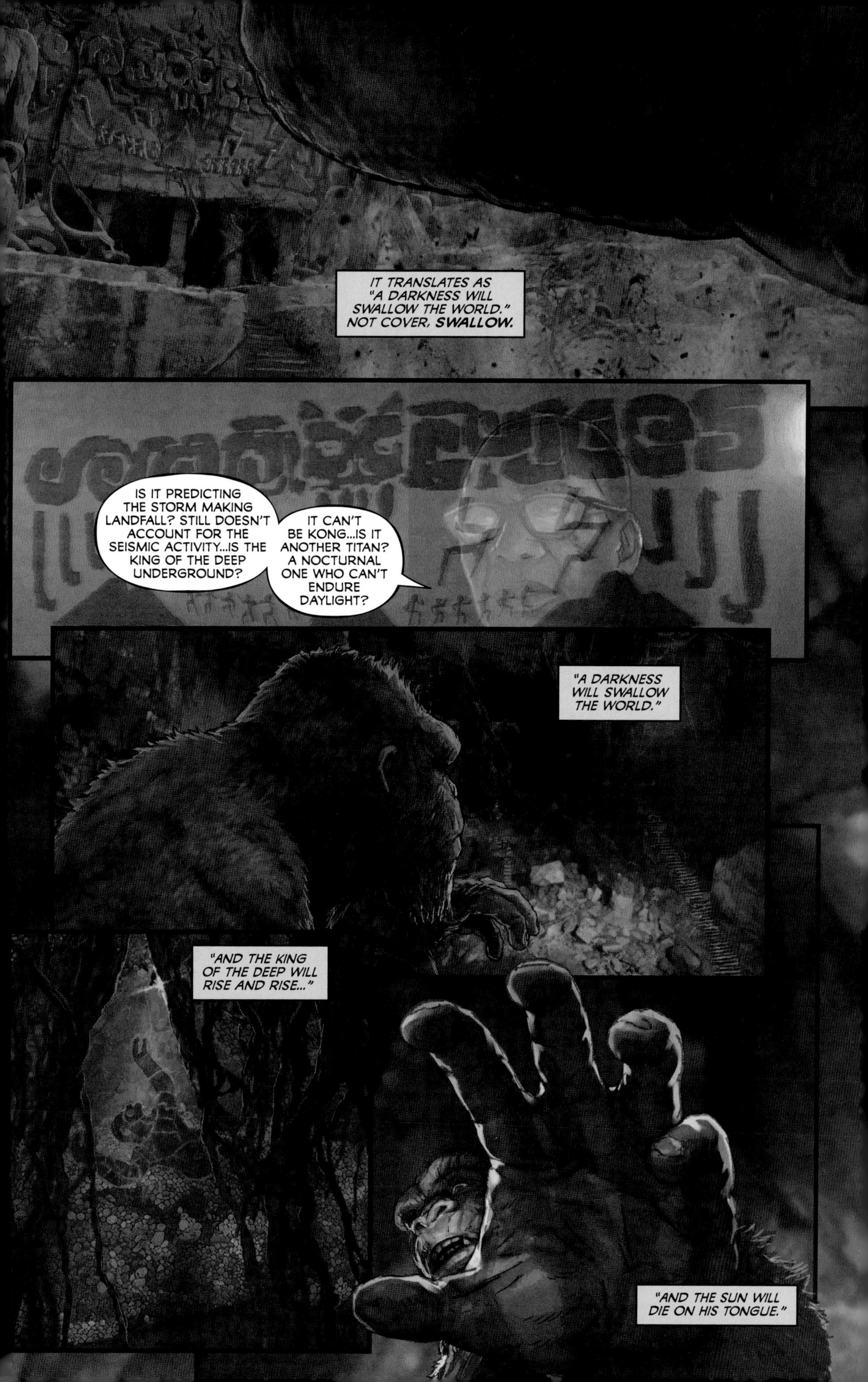
IT TRANSLATES AS "A DARKNESS WILL SWALLOW THE WORLD." NOT COVER, **SWALLOW.**
IS IT PREDICTING THE STORM MAKING LANDFALL? STILL DOESN'T ACCOUNT FOR THE SEISMIC ACTIVITY...IS THE KING OF THE DEEP UNDERGROUND?
IT CAN'T BE KONG...IS IT ANOTHER TITAN? A NOCTURNAL ONE WHO CAN'T ENDURE DAYLIGHT?
"A DARKNESS WILL SWALLOW THE WORLD."
"AND THE KING OF THE DEEP WILL RISE AND RISE..."
"AND THE SUN WILL DIE ON HIS TONGUE."

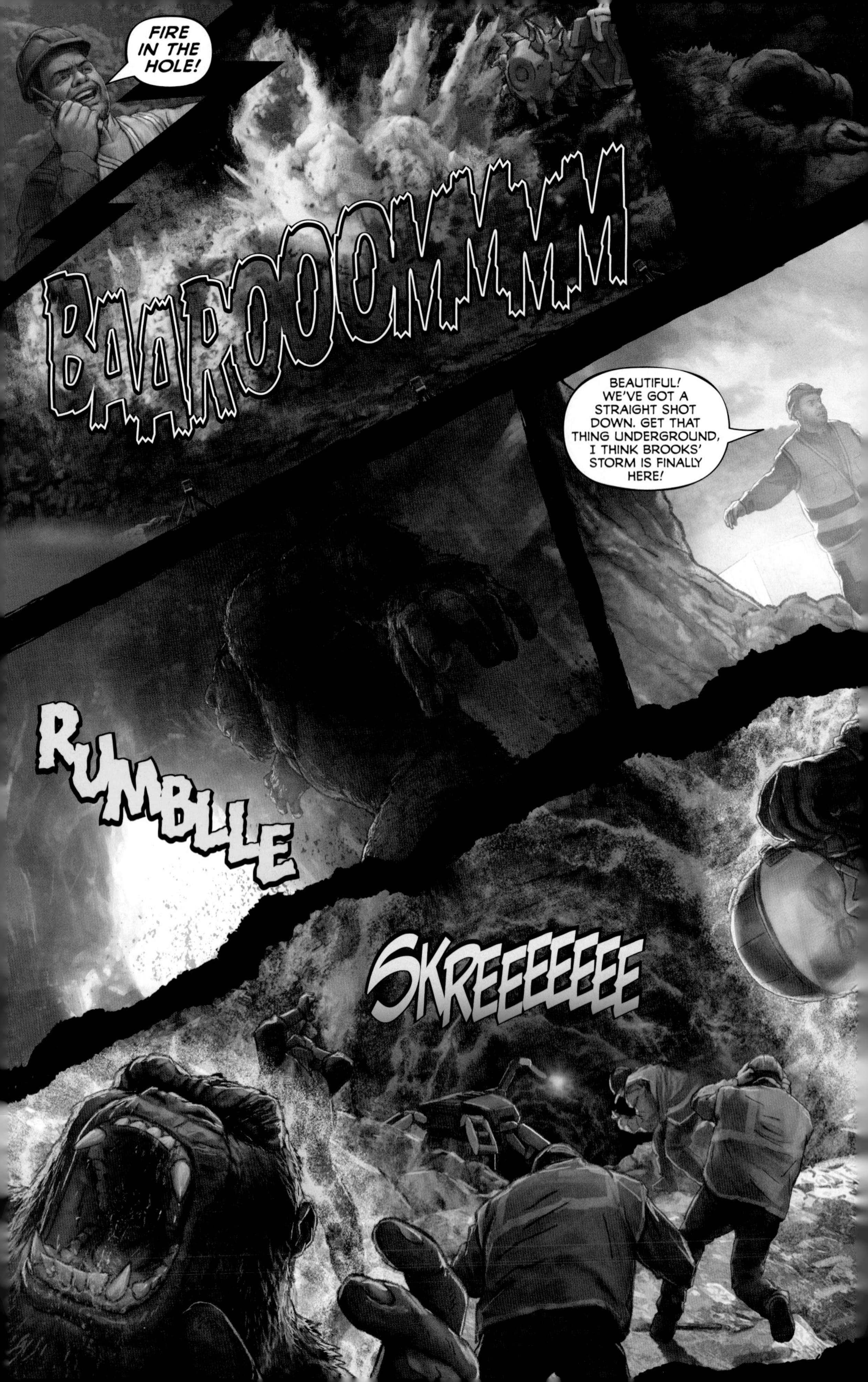
FIRE IN THE HOLE!
BAAROOOMMMM
BEAUTIFUL! WE'VE GOT A STRAIGHT SHOT DOWN. GET THAT THING UNDERGROUND, I THINK BROOKS' STORM IS FINALLY HERE!
RUMBLLE
SKREEEEEEE

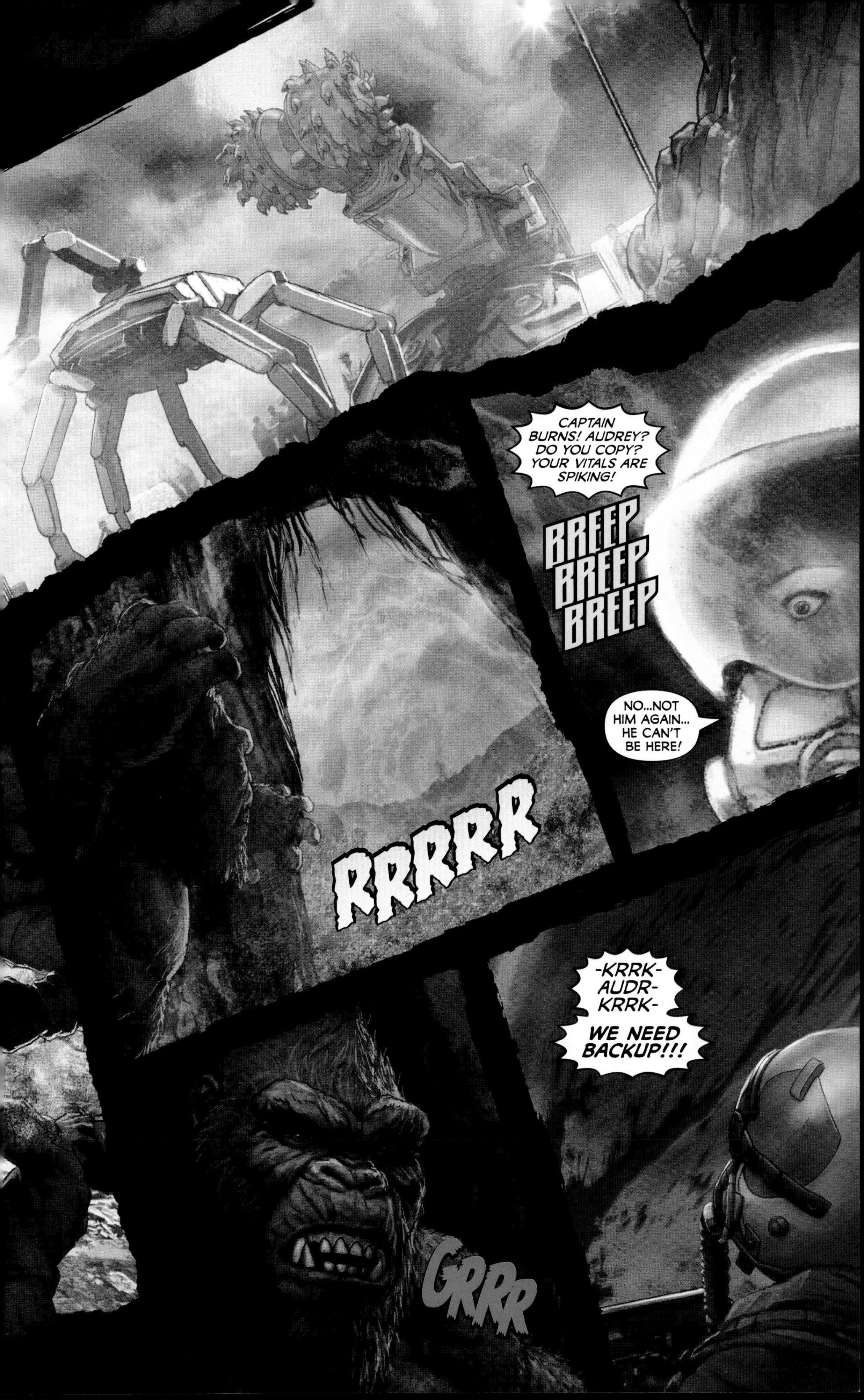
CAPTAIN BURNS! AUDREY? DO YOU COPY? YOUR VITALS ARE SPIKING!
BREEP BREEP BREEP
NO...NOT HIM AGAIN... HE CAN'T BE HERE!
RRRRR
-KRRK- AUDR- KRRK-
WE NEED BACKUP!!!
GRRR

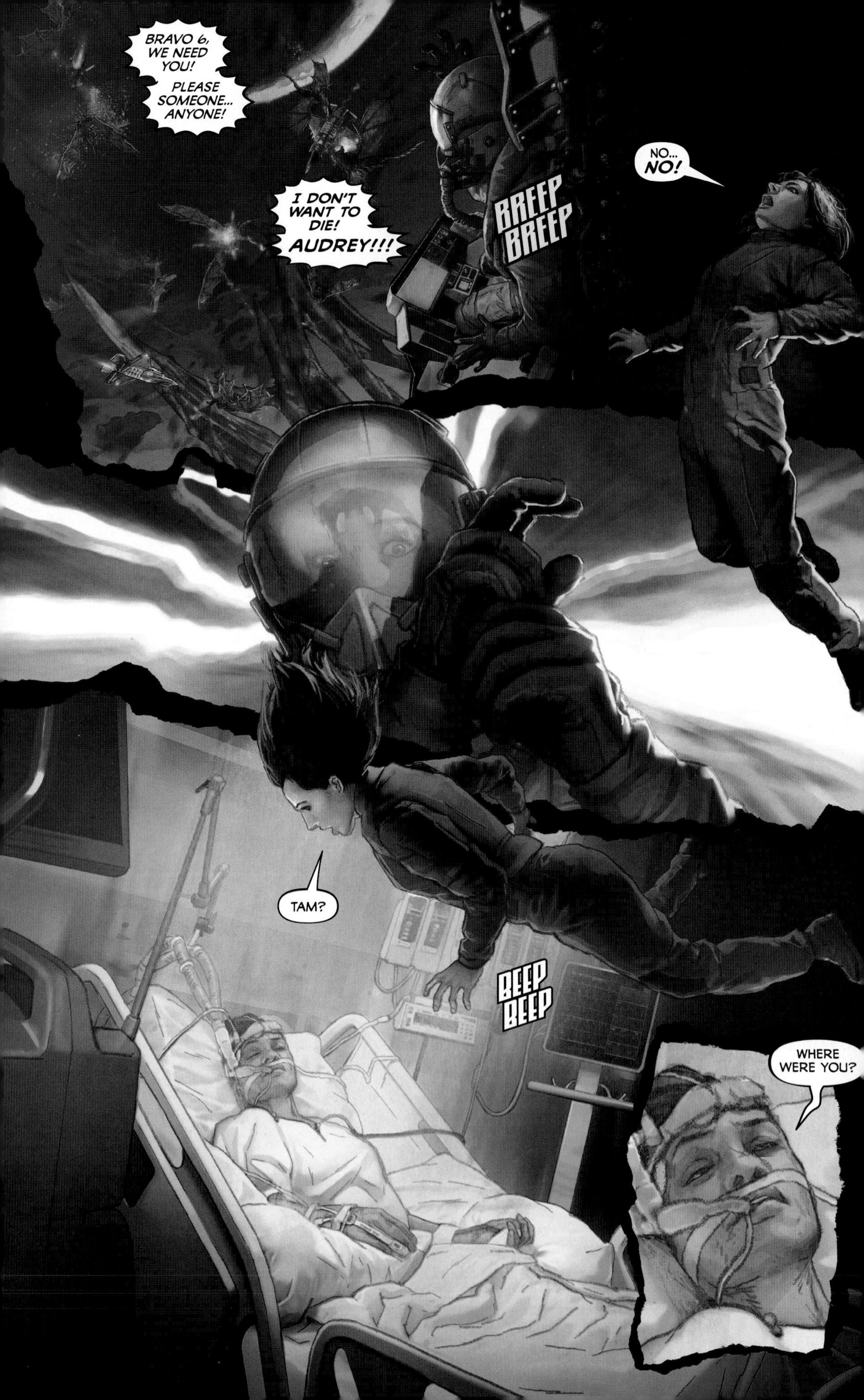
BRAVO 6, WE NEED YOU!
PLEASE SOMEONE... ANYONE!
I DON'T WANT TO DIE! AUDREY!!!
BREEP BREEP
NO... NO!
TAM?
BEEP BEEP
WHERE WERE YOU?

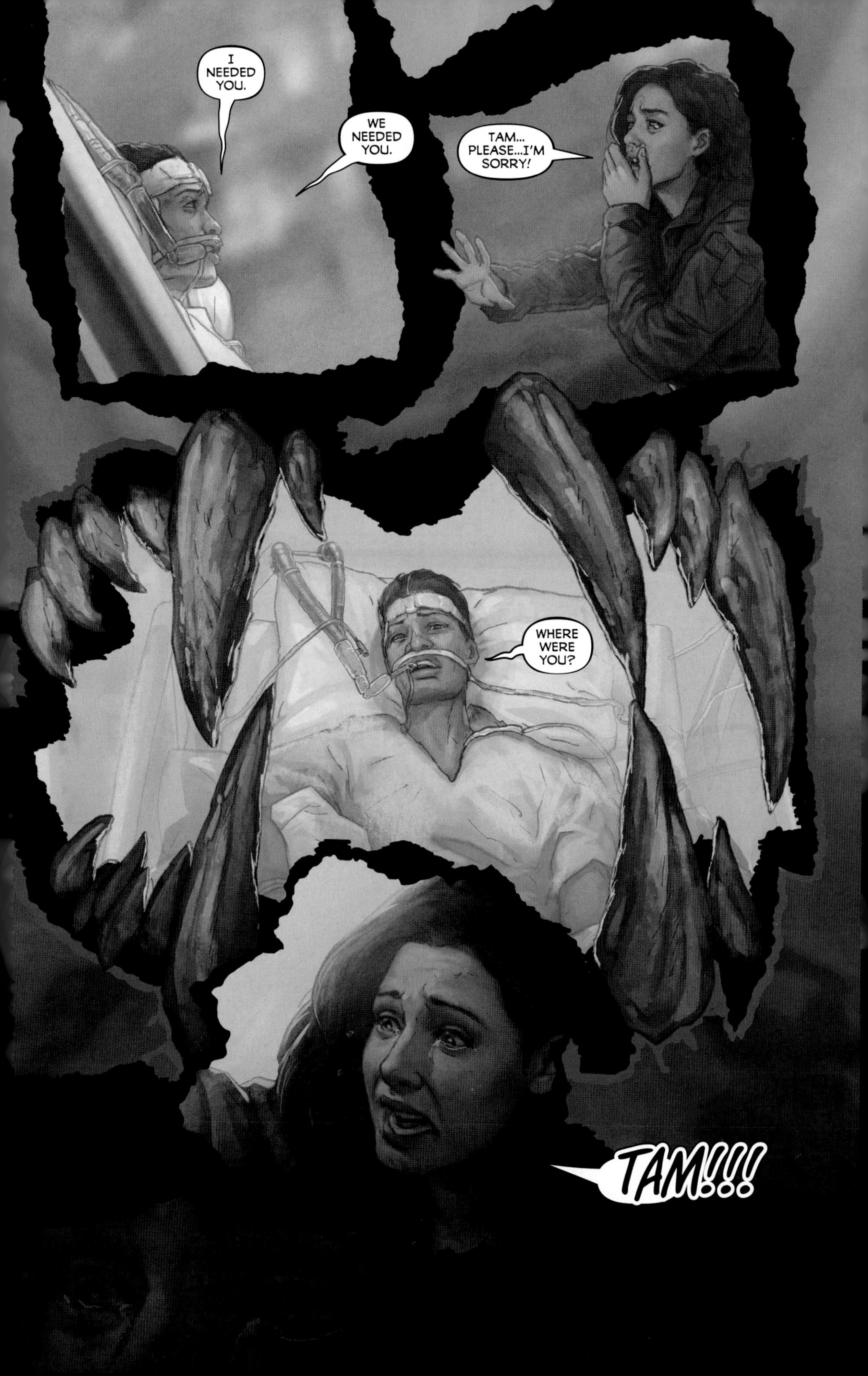
I NEEDED YOU.
WE NEEDED YOU.
TAM... PLEASE...I'M SORRY!
WHERE WERE YOU?
TAM!!!

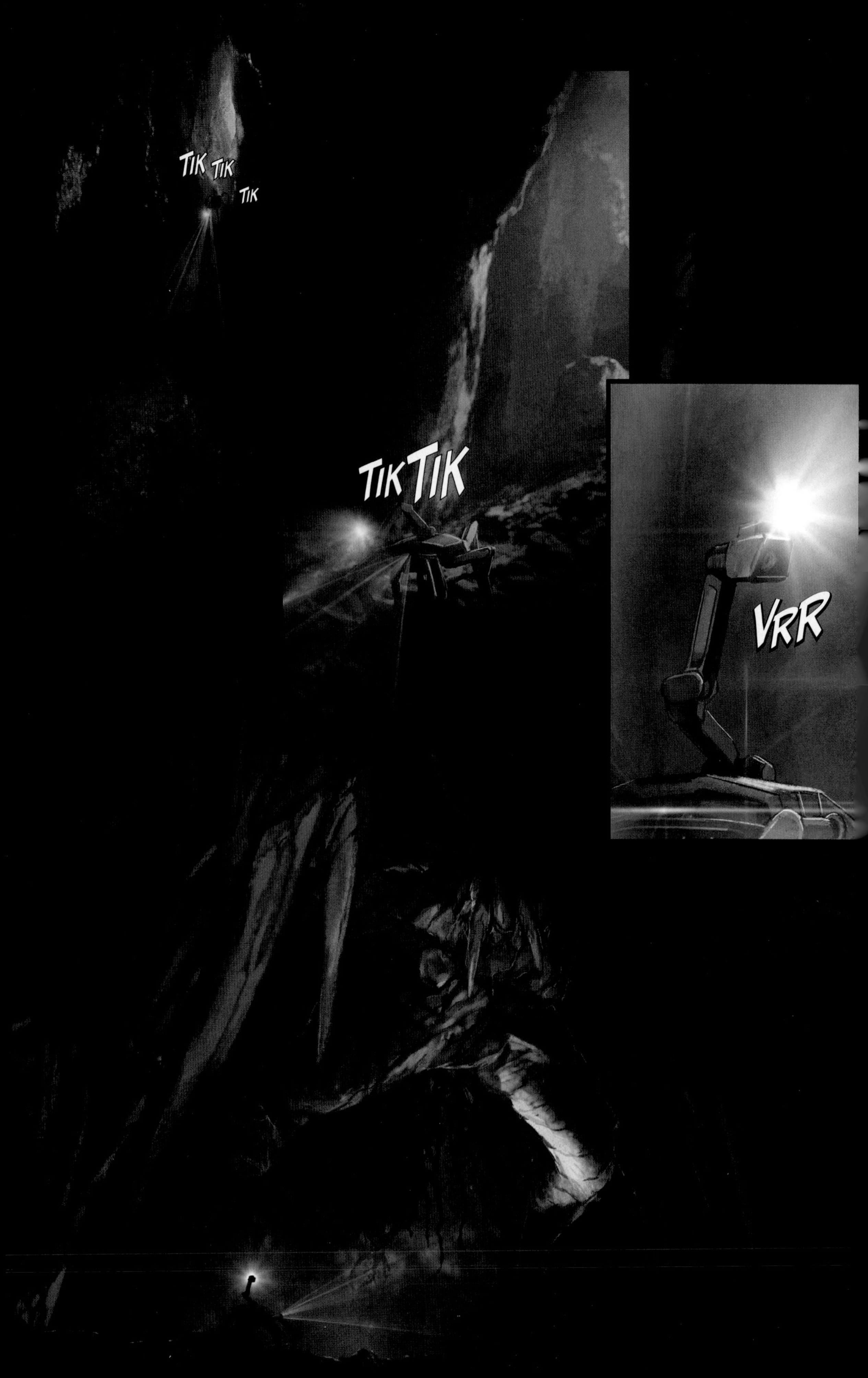

TIK TIK
TIK
TIK TIK
VRR

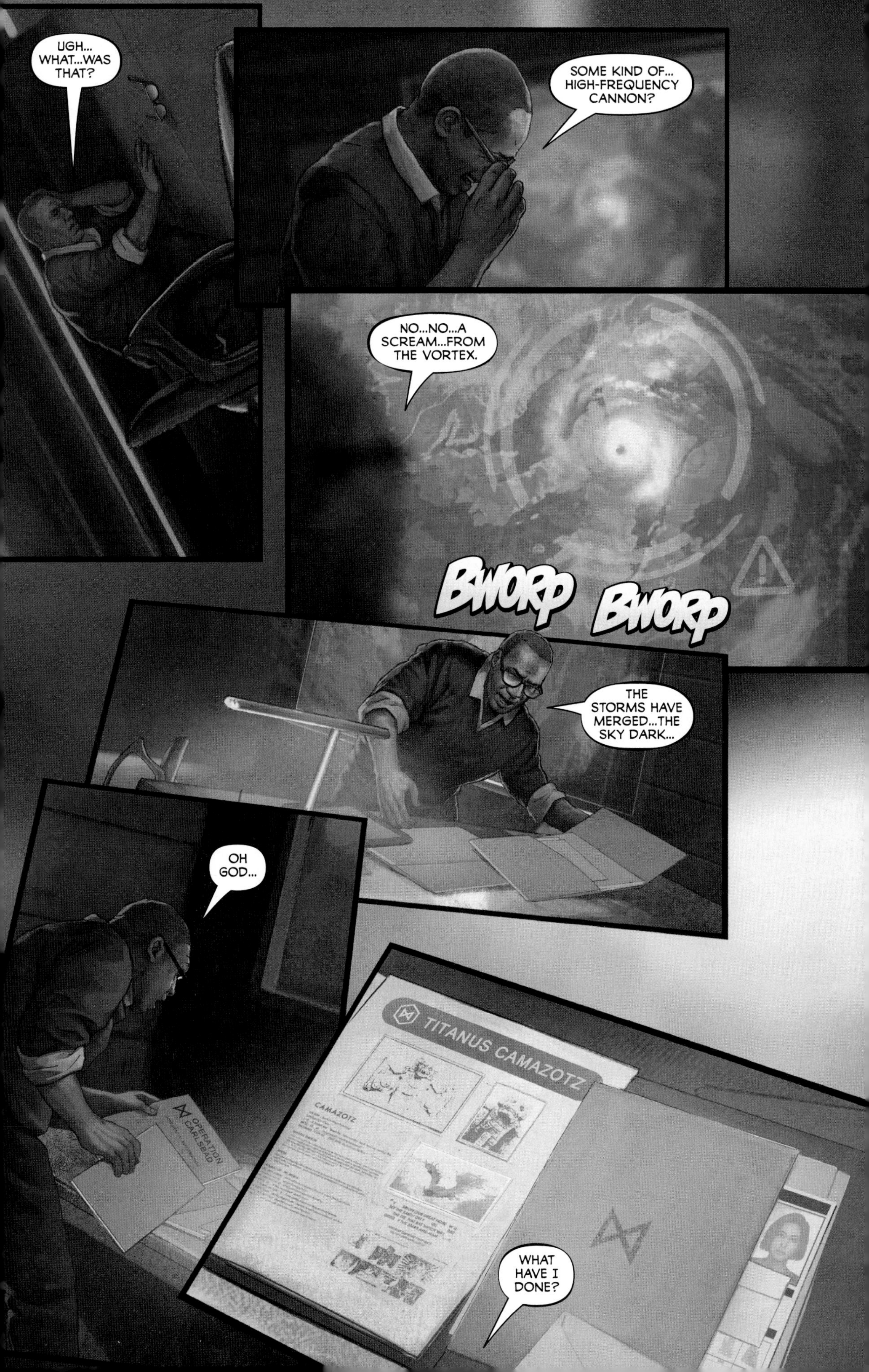
UGH... WHAT...WAS THAT?
SOME KIND OF... HIGH-FREQUENCY CANNON?
NO...NO...A SCREAM...FROM THE VORTEX.
BWORP BWORP
THE STORMS HAVE MERGED...THE SKY DARK...
OH GOD...
OPERATION CARLSBAD
TITANUS CAMAZOTZ
CAMAZOTZ
WHAT HAVE I DONE?

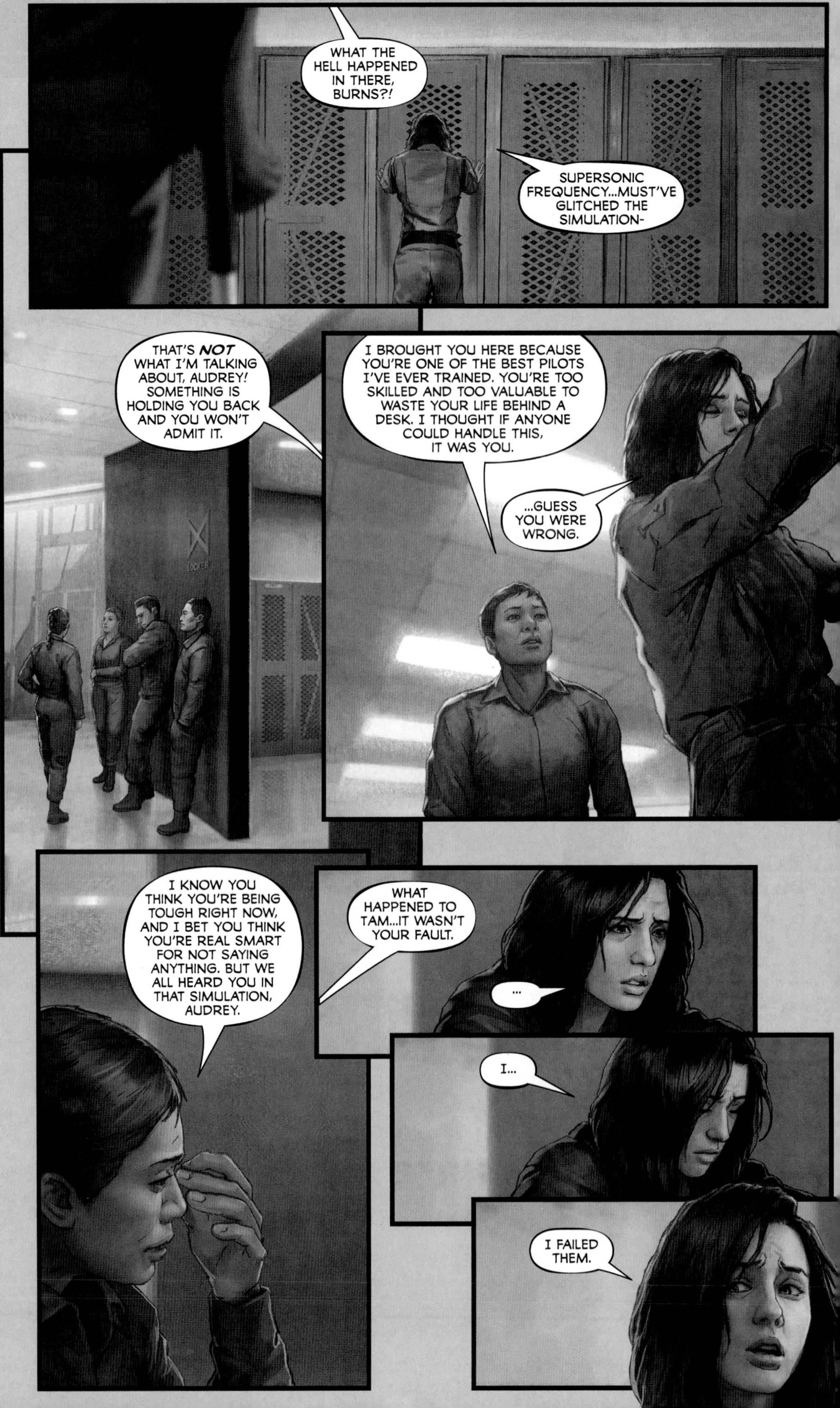
WHAT THE HELL HAPPENED IN THERE, BURNS?!
SUPERSONIC FREQUENCY...MUST'VE GLITCHED THE SIMULATION-
THAT'S NOT WHAT I'M TALKING ABOUT, AUDREY! SOMETHING IS HOLDING YOU BACK AND YOU WON'T ADMIT IT.
I BROUGHT YOU HERE BECAUSE YOU'RE ONE OF THE BEST PILOTS I'VE EVER TRAINED. YOU'RE TOO SKILLED AND TOO VALUABLE TO WASTE YOUR LIFE BEHIND A DESK. I THOUGHT IF ANYONE COULD HANDLE THIS, IT WAS YOU.
...GUESS YOU WERE WRONG.
I KNOW YOU THINK YOU'RE BEING TOUGH RIGHT NOW, AND I BET YOU THINK YOU'RE REAL SMART FOR NOT SAYING ANYTHING. BUT WE ALL HEARD YOU IN THAT SIMULATION, AUDREY.
WHAT HAPPENED TO TAM...IT WASN'T YOUR FAULT.
...
I...
I FAILED THEM.

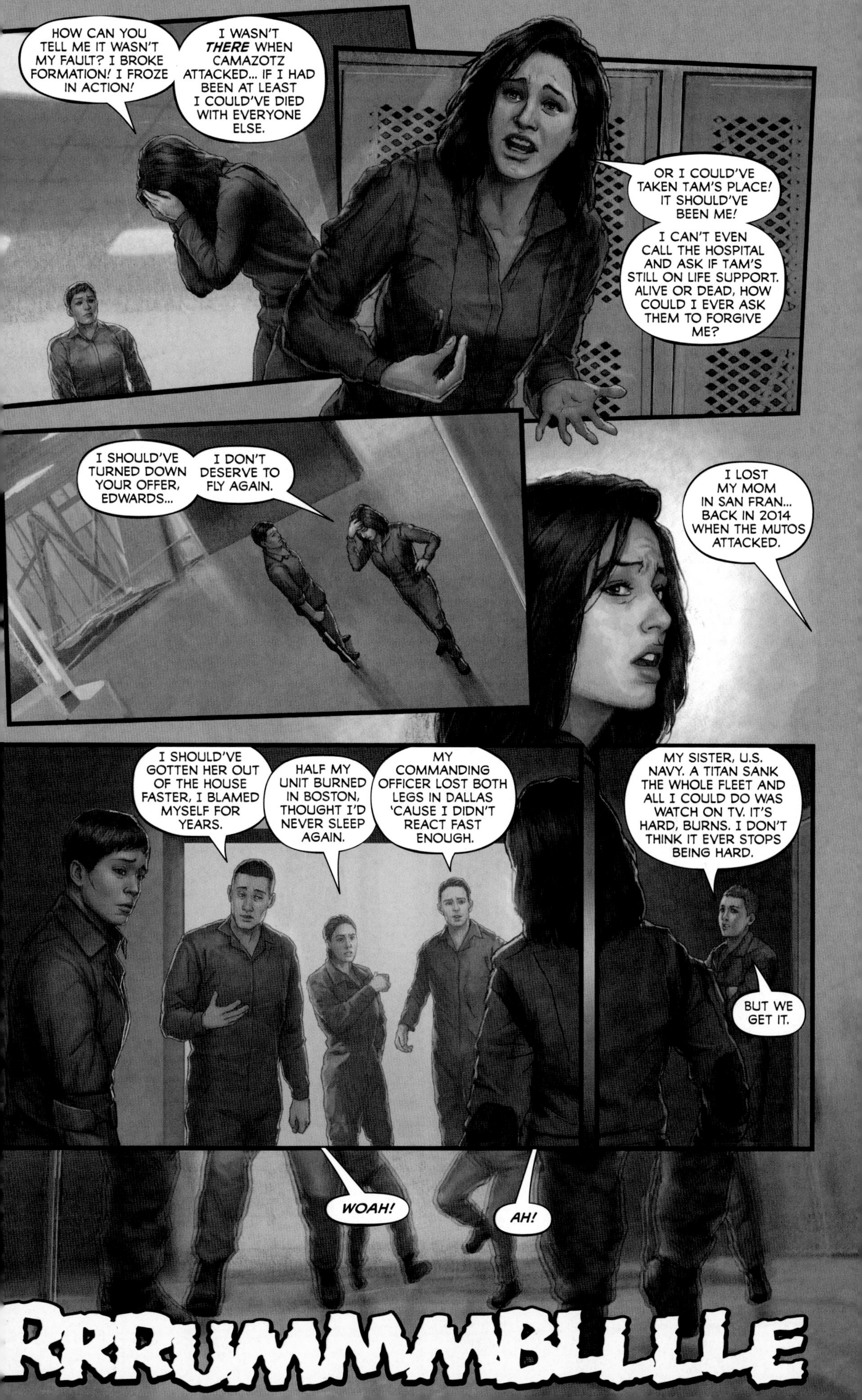
HOW CAN YOU TELL ME IT WASN'T MY FAULT? I BROKE FORMATION! I FROZE IN ACTION!
I WASN'T *THERE* WHEN CAMAZOTZ ATTACKED... IF I HAD BEEN AT LEAST I COULD'VE DIED WITH EVERYONE ELSE.
OR I COULD'VE TAKEN TAM'S PLACE! IT SHOULD'VE BEEN ME!
I CAN'T EVEN CALL THE HOSPITAL AND ASK IF TAM'S STILL ON LIFE SUPPORT. ALIVE OR DEAD, HOW COULD I EVER ASK THEM TO FORGIVE ME?
I SHOULD'VE TURNED DOWN YOUR OFFER, EDWARDS...
I DON'T DESERVE TO FLY AGAIN.
I LOST MY MOM IN SAN FRAN... BACK IN 2014 WHEN THE MUTOS ATTACKED.
I SHOULD'VE GOTTEN HER OUT OF THE HOUSE FASTER, I BLAMED MYSELF FOR YEARS.
HALF MY UNIT BURNED IN BOSTON, THOUGHT I'D NEVER SLEEP AGAIN.
MY COMMANDING OFFICER LOST BOTH LEGS IN DALLAS 'CAUSE I DIDN'T REACT FAST ENOUGH.
MY SISTER, U.S. NAVY. A TITAN SANK THE WHOLE FLEET AND ALL I COULD DO WAS WATCH ON TV. IT'S HARD, BURNS. I DON'T THINK IT EVER STOPS BEING HARD.
BUT WE GET IT.
WOAH!
AH!
RRRUMMMBLLLE

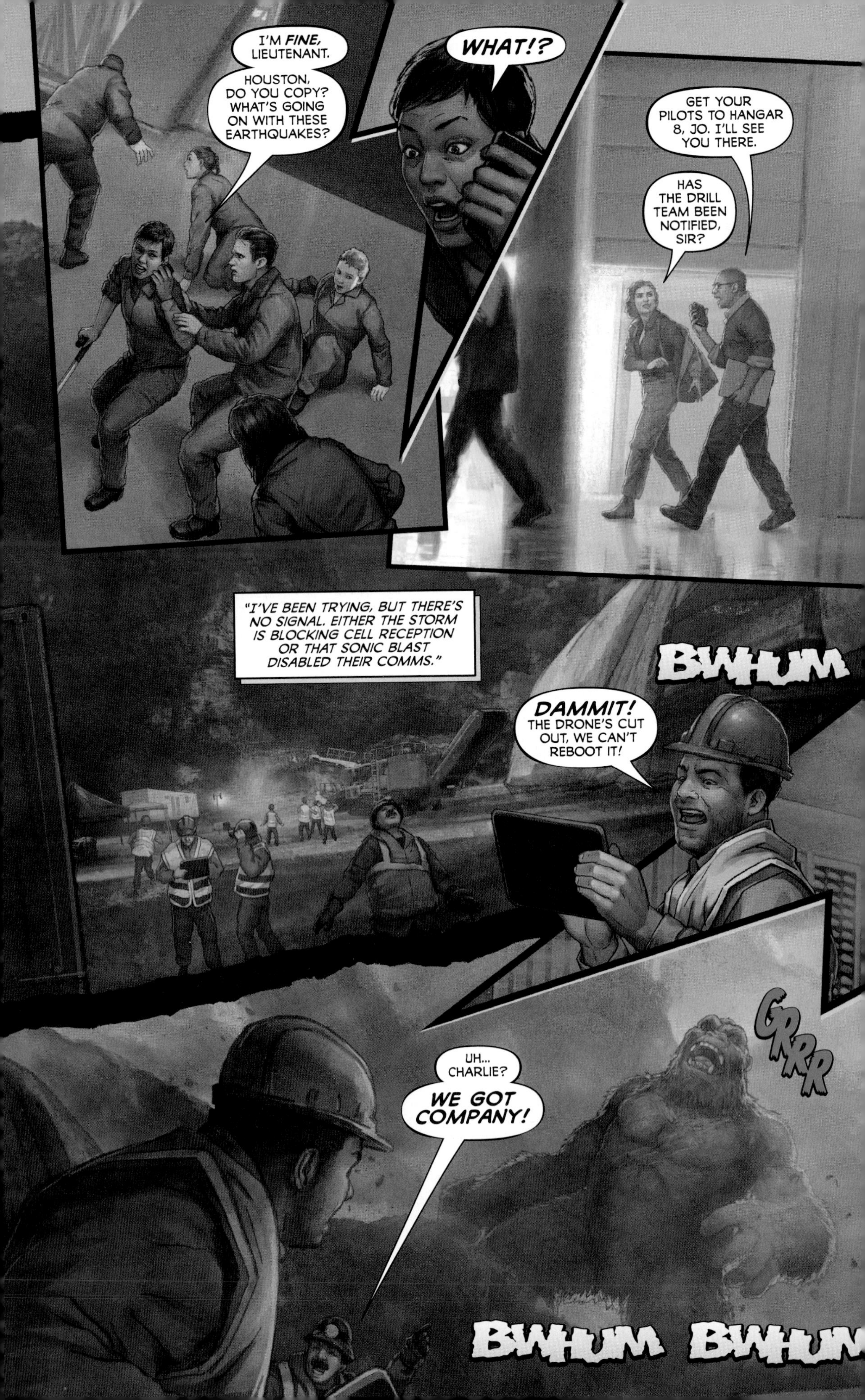
I'M FINE, LIEUTENANT.
HOUSTON, DO YOU COPY? WHAT'S GOING ON WITH THESE EARTHQUAKES?
WHAT!?
GET YOUR PILOTS TO HANGAR 8, JO. I'LL SEE YOU THERE.
HAS THE DRILL TEAM BEEN NOTIFIED, SIR?
"I'VE BEEN TRYING, BUT THERE'S NO SIGNAL. EITHER THE STORM IS BLOCKING CELL RECEPTION OR THAT SONIC BLAST DISABLED THEIR COMMS."
BWHUM
DAMMIT! THE DRONE'S CUT OUT, WE CAN'T REBOOT IT!
GRRR
UH... CHARLIE?
WE GOT COMPANY!
BWHUM BWHUM

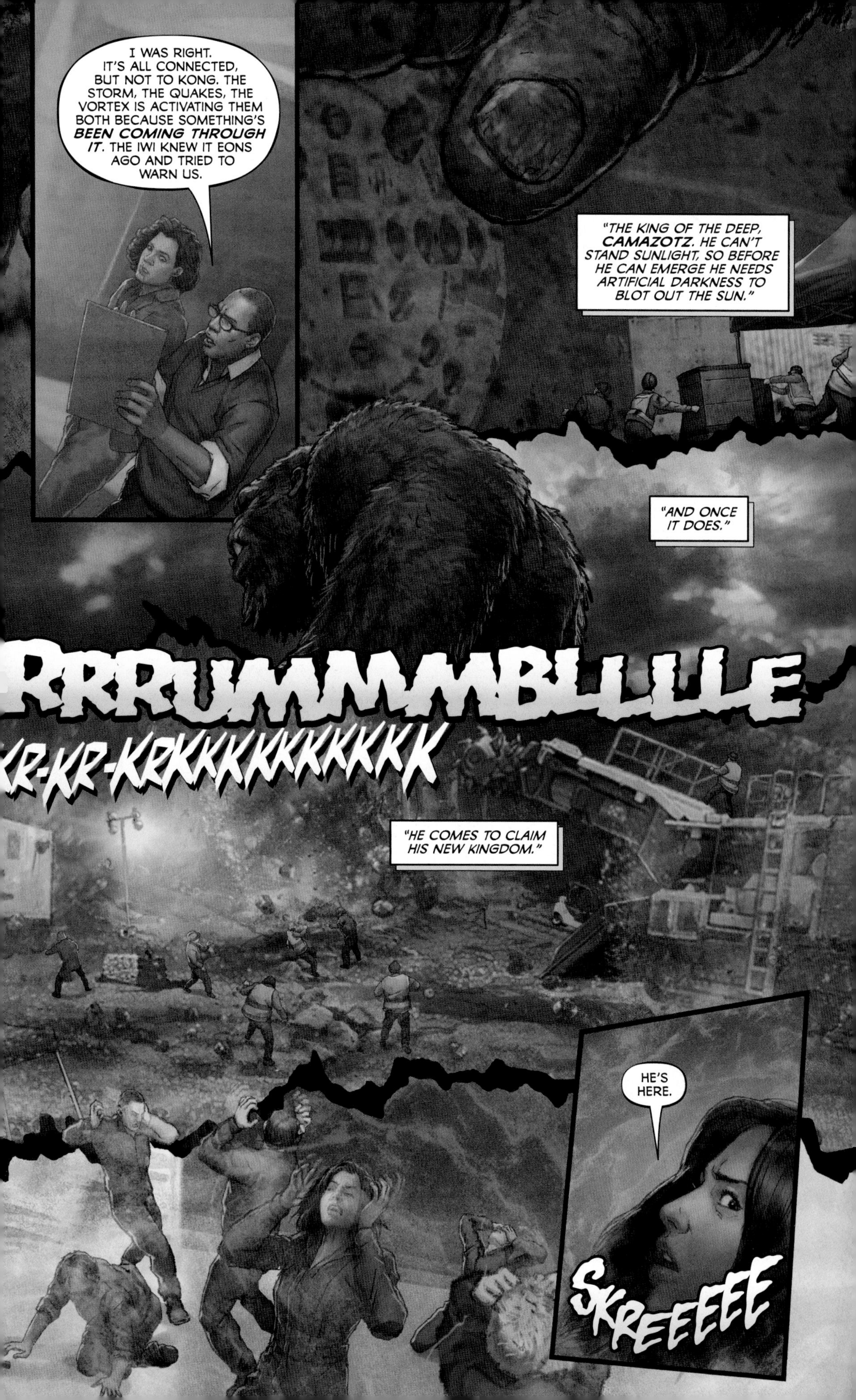
I WAS RIGHT. IT'S ALL CONNECTED, BUT NOT TO KONG. THE STORM, THE QUAKES, THE VORTEX IS ACTIVATING THEM BOTH BECAUSE SOMETHING'S ***BEEN COMING THROUGH IT***. THE IWI KNEW IT EONS AGO AND TRIED TO WARN US.
"THE KING OF THE DEEP, ***CAMAZOTZ***. HE CAN'T STAND SUNLIGHT, SO BEFORE HE CAN EMERGE HE NEEDS ARTIFICIAL DARKNESS TO BLOT OUT THE SUN."
"AND ONCE IT DOES."
RRRUMMMBLLLE
KR-KR-KRKKKKKKKKK
"HE COMES TO CLAIM HIS NEW KINGDOM."
HE'S HERE.
SKREEEEEE

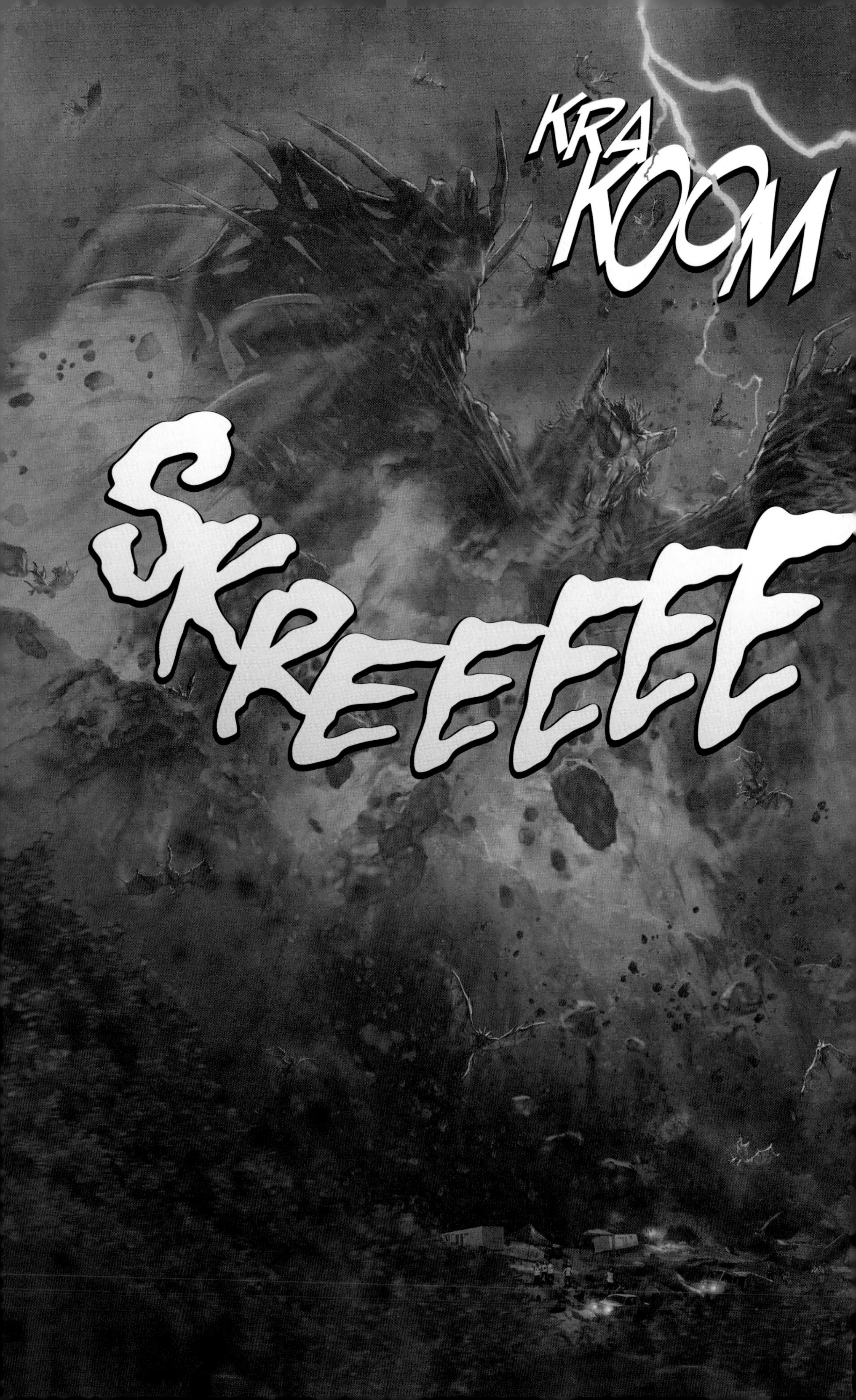
KRA
KOOM
SKREEEEE

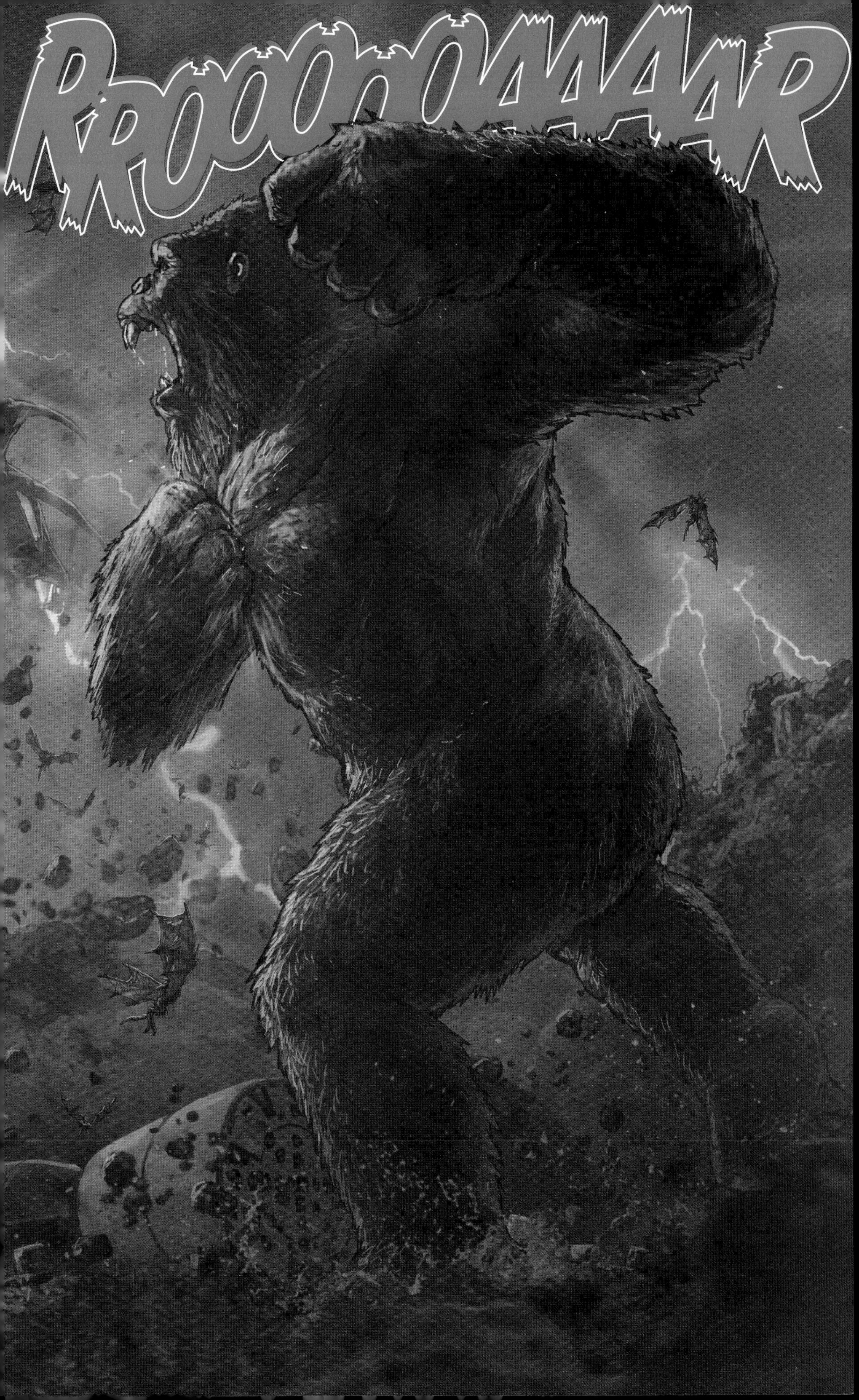
RROOOOOAAAAR

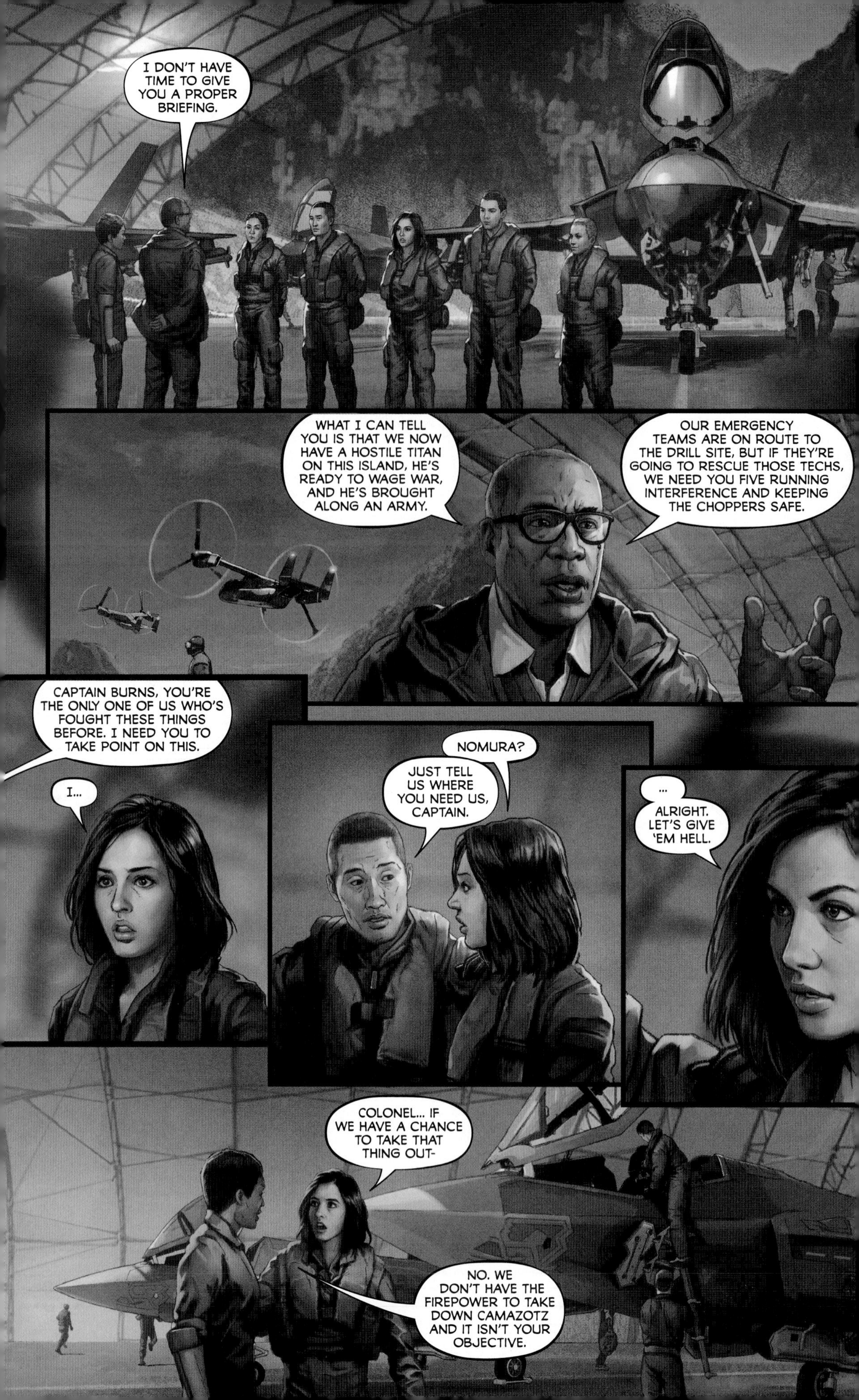

I DON'T HAVE TIME TO GIVE YOU A PROPER BRIEFING.
WHAT I CAN TELL YOU IS THAT WE NOW HAVE A HOSTILE TITAN ON THIS ISLAND, HE'S READY TO WAGE WAR, AND HE'S BROUGHT ALONG AN ARMY.
OUR EMERGENCY TEAMS ARE ON ROUTE TO THE DRILL SITE, BUT IF THEY'RE GOING TO RESCUE THOSE TECHS, WE NEED YOU FIVE RUNNING INTERFERENCE AND KEEPING THE CHOPPERS SAFE.
CAPTAIN BURNS, YOU'RE THE ONLY ONE OF US WHO'S FOUGHT THESE THINGS BEFORE. I NEED YOU TO TAKE POINT ON THIS.
I...
NOMURA?
JUST TELL US WHERE YOU NEED US, CAPTAIN.
...
ALRIGHT. LET'S GIVE 'EM HELL.
COLONEL... IF WE HAVE A CHANCE TO TAKE THAT THING OUT-
NO. WE DON'T HAVE THE FIREPOWER TO TAKE DOWN CAMAZOTZ AND IT ISN'T YOUR OBJECTIVE.

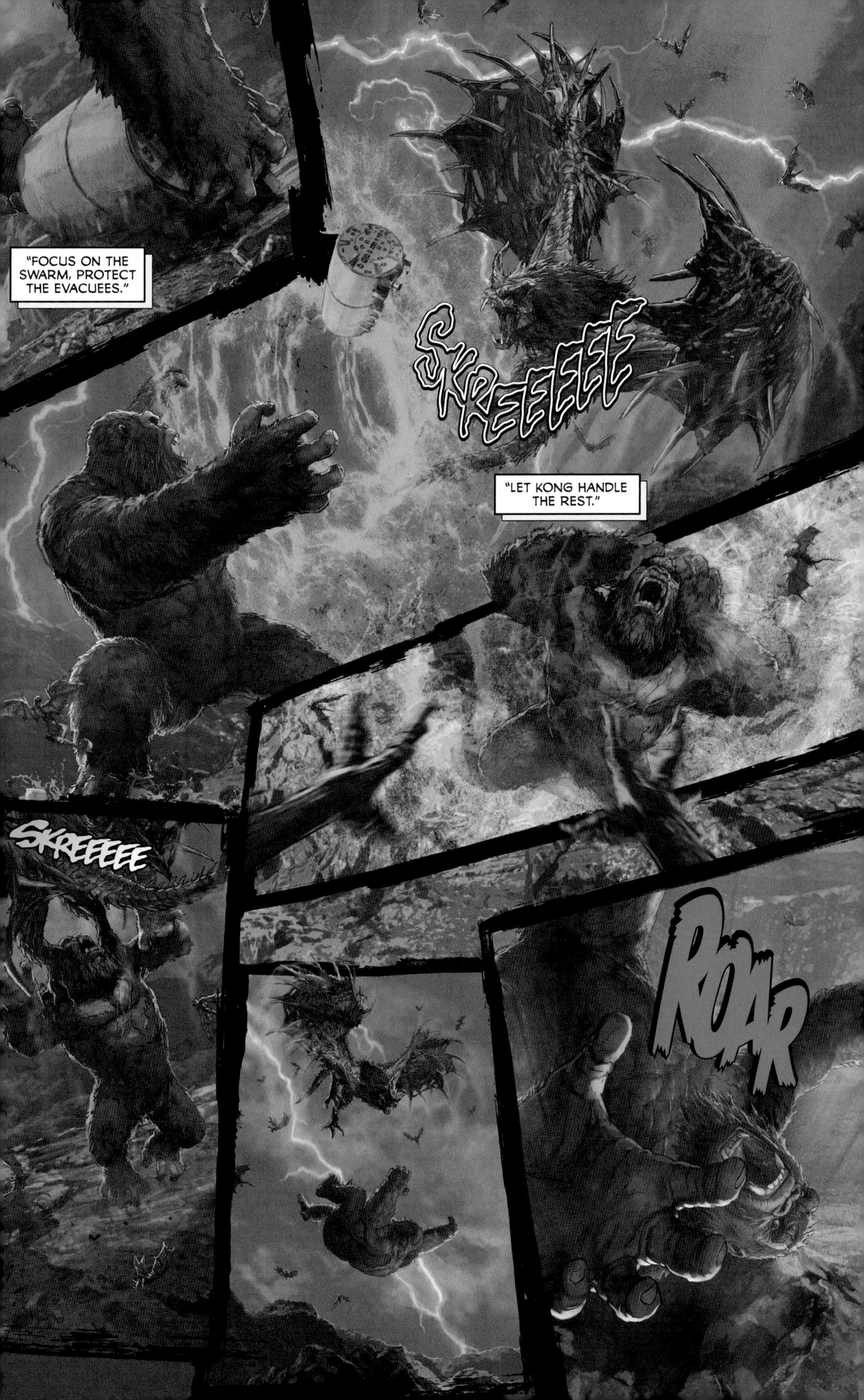

"FOCUS ON THE SWARM, PROTECT THE EVACUEES."
SKREEEEEE
"LET KONG HANDLE THE REST."
SKREEEEEE
ROAR

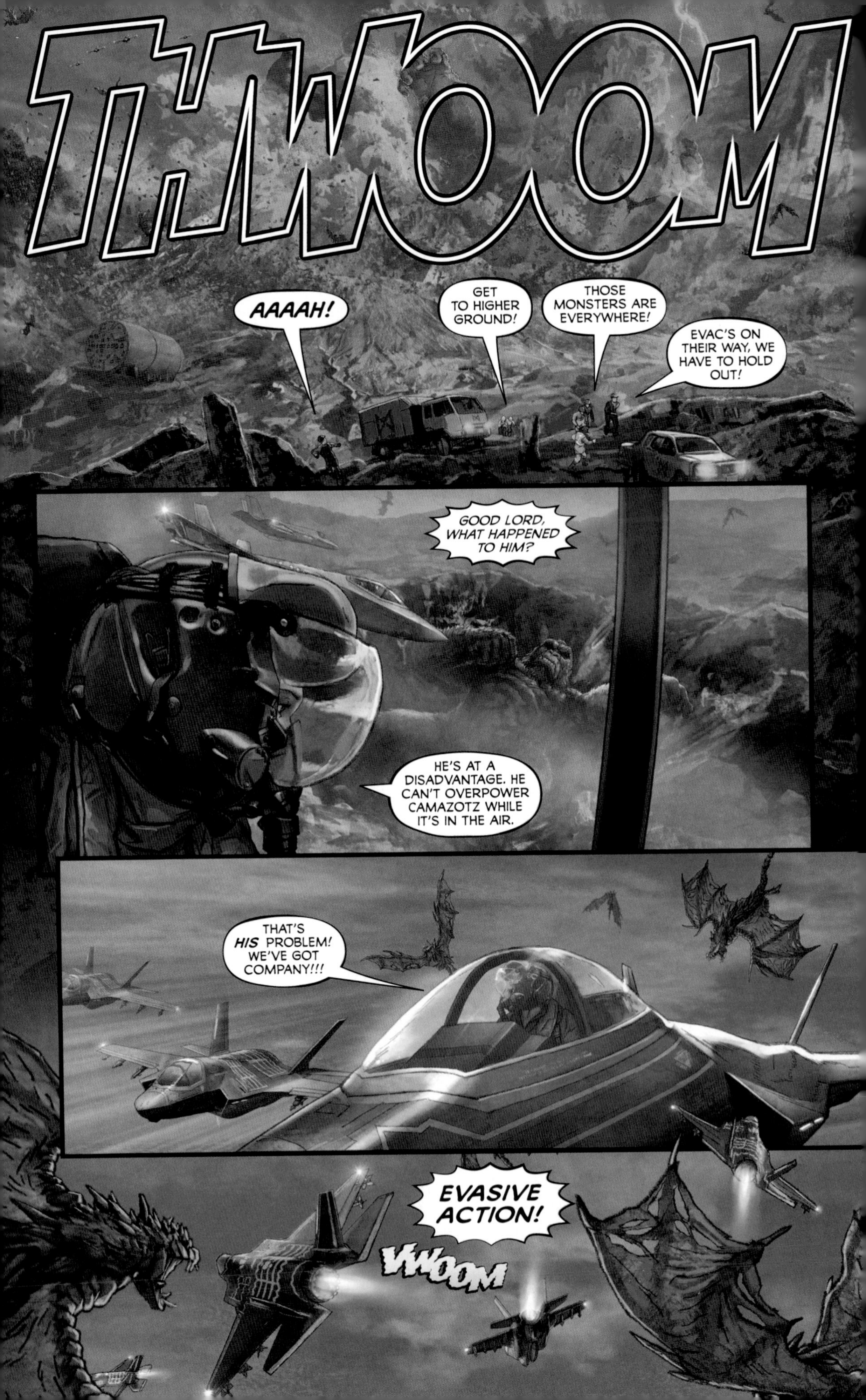
THWOOM
AAAAH!
GET TO HIGHER GROUND!
THOSE MONSTERS ARE EVERYWHERE!
EVAC'S ON THEIR WAY, WE HAVE TO HOLD OUT!
GOOD LORD, WHAT HAPPENED TO HIM?
HE'S AT A DISADVANTAGE. HE CAN'T OVERPOWER CAMAZOTZ WHILE IT'S IN THE AIR.
THAT'S HIS PROBLEM! WE'VE GOT COMPANY!!!
EVASIVE ACTION!
VWOOM

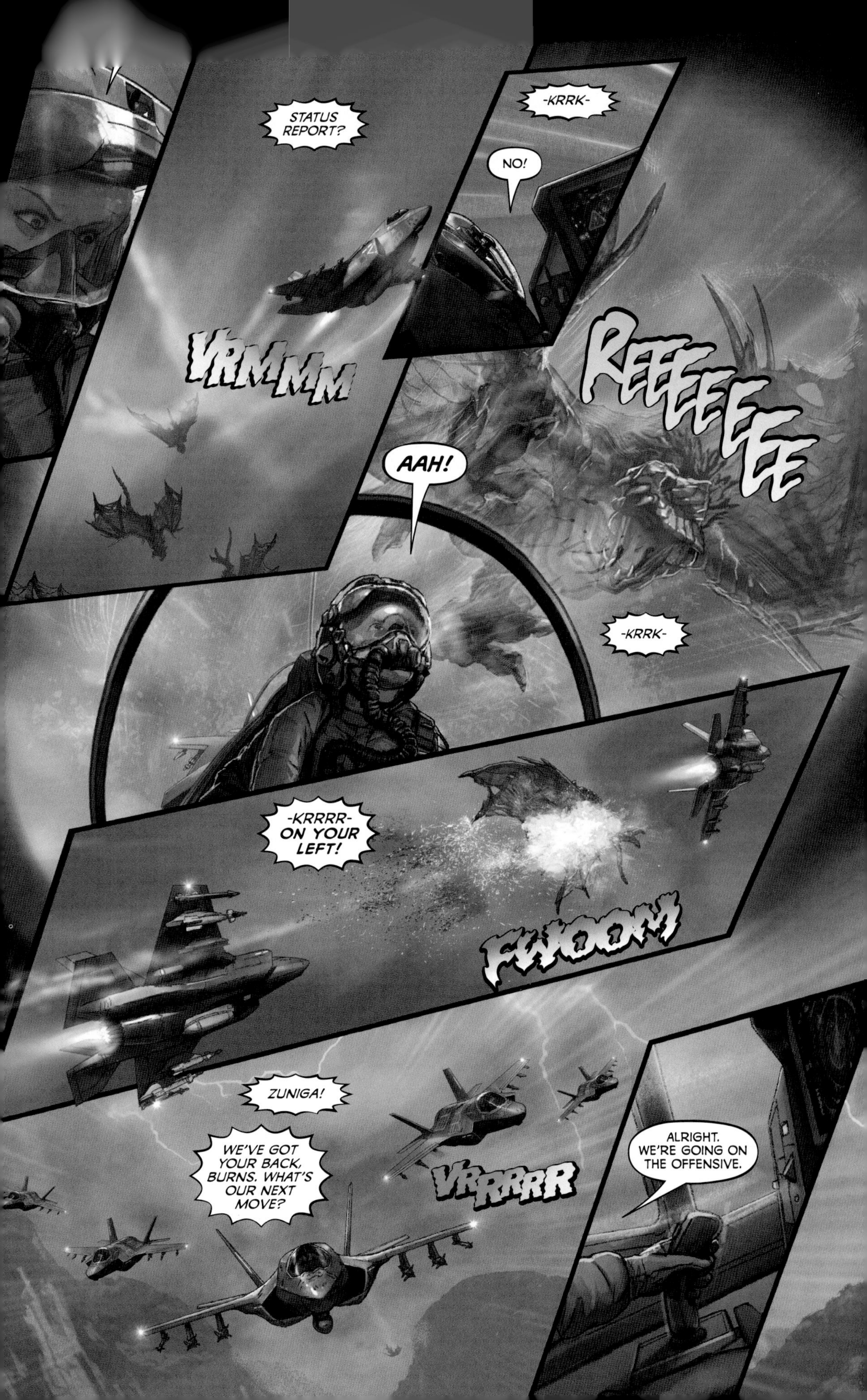
STATUS REPORT?
VRMMMM
-KRRK-
NO!
REEEEEEEE
AAH!
-KRRK-
-KRRRR- ON YOUR LEFT!
FWOOM
ZUNIGA!
WE'VE GOT YOUR BACK, BURNS. WHAT'S OUR NEXT MOVE?
VRRRRR
ALRIGHT. WE'RE GOING ON THE OFFENSIVE.

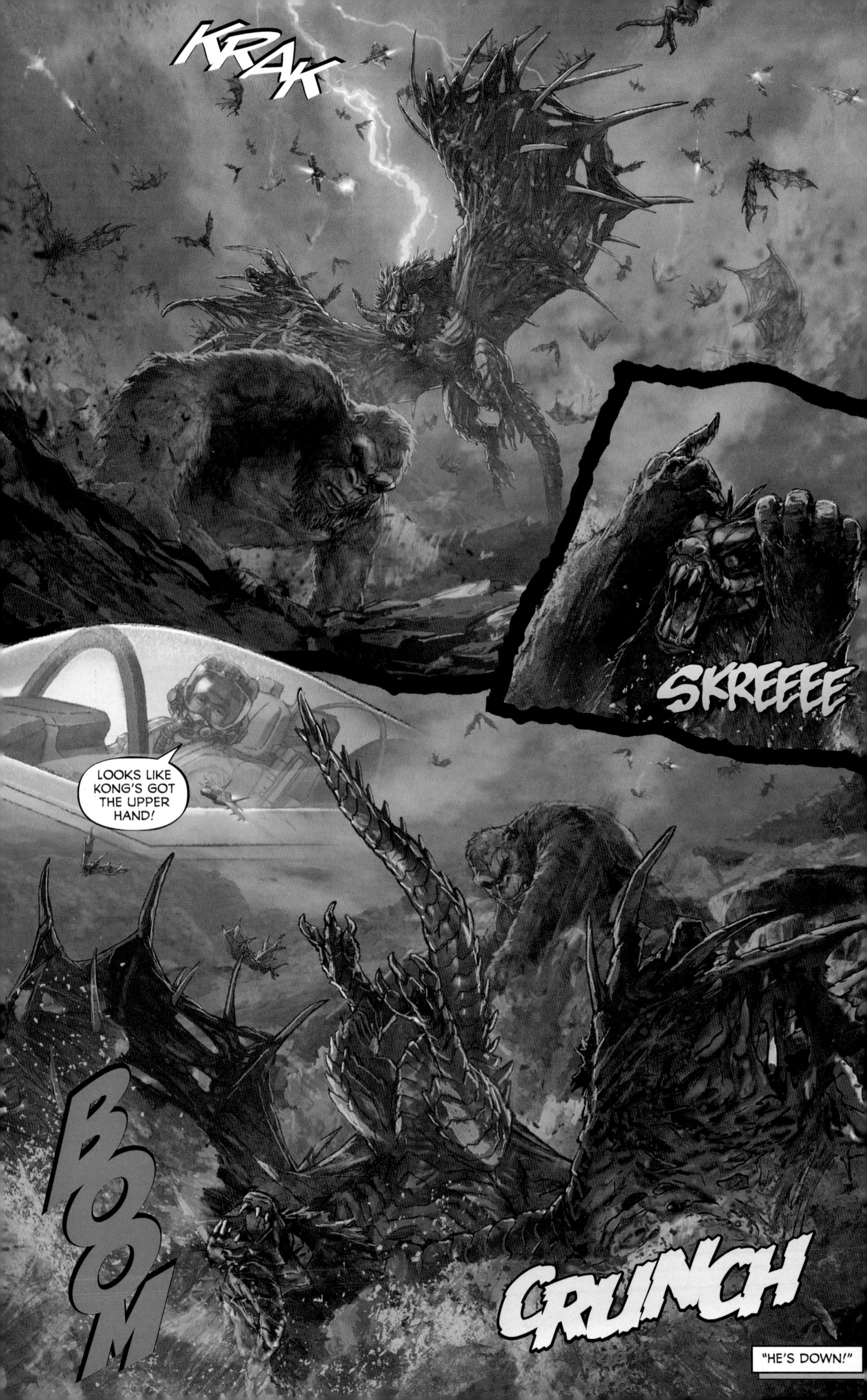
KRAK
SKREEEE
LOOKS LIKE KONG'S GOT THE UPPER HAND!
BOOM
CRUNCH
"HE'S DOWN!"

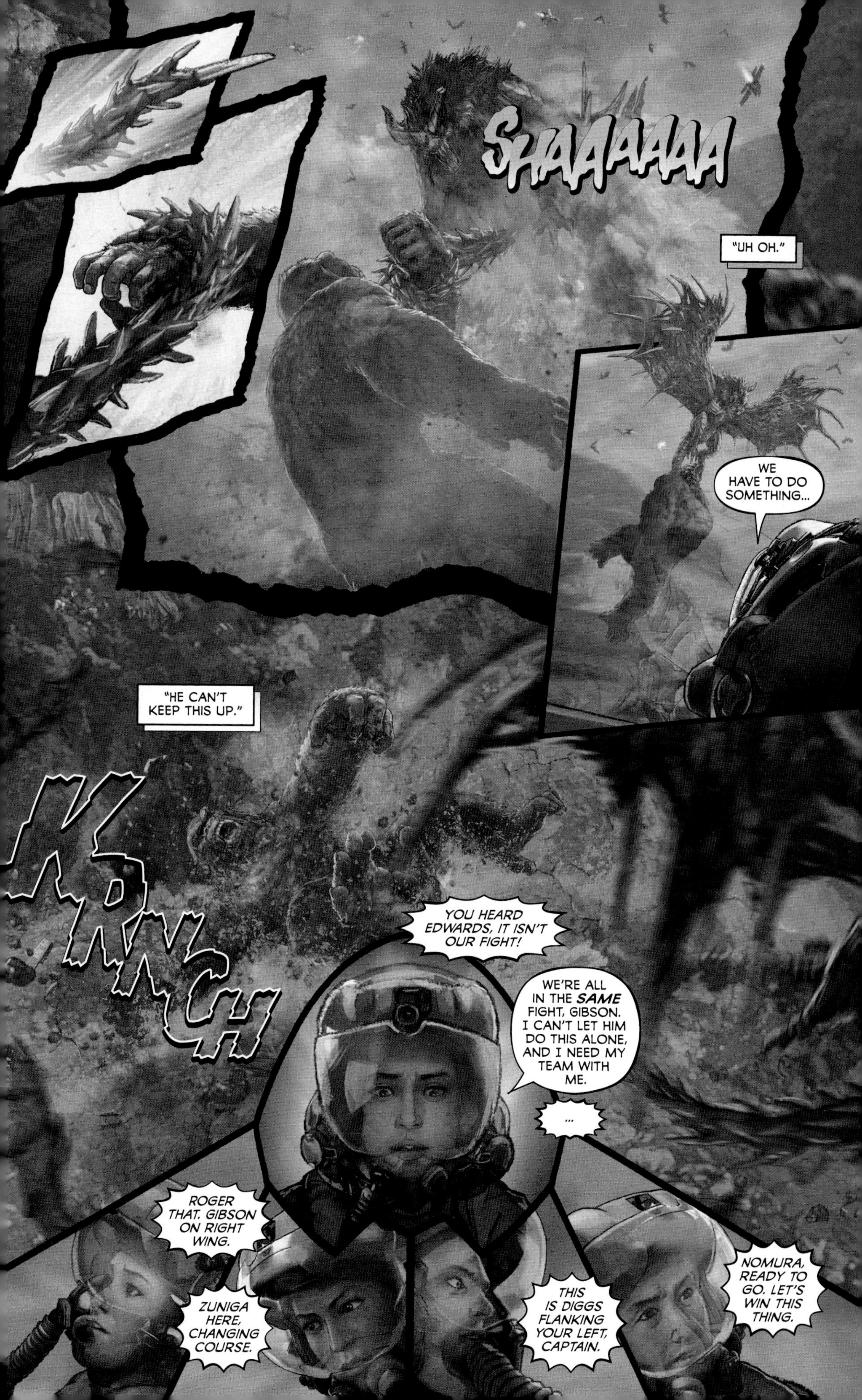
SHAAAAAA
"UH OH."
WE HAVE TO DO SOMETHING...
"HE CAN'T KEEP THIS UP."
KRRNCH
YOU HEARD EDWARDS, IT ISN'T OUR FIGHT!
WE'RE ALL IN THE SAME FIGHT, GIBSON. I CAN'T LET HIM DO THIS ALONE, AND I NEED MY TEAM WITH ME.
...
ROGER THAT. GIBSON ON RIGHT WING.
ZUNIGA HERE, CHANGING COURSE.
THIS IS DIGGS FLANKING YOUR LEFT, CAPTAIN.
NOMURA, READY TO GO. LET'S WIN THIS THING.

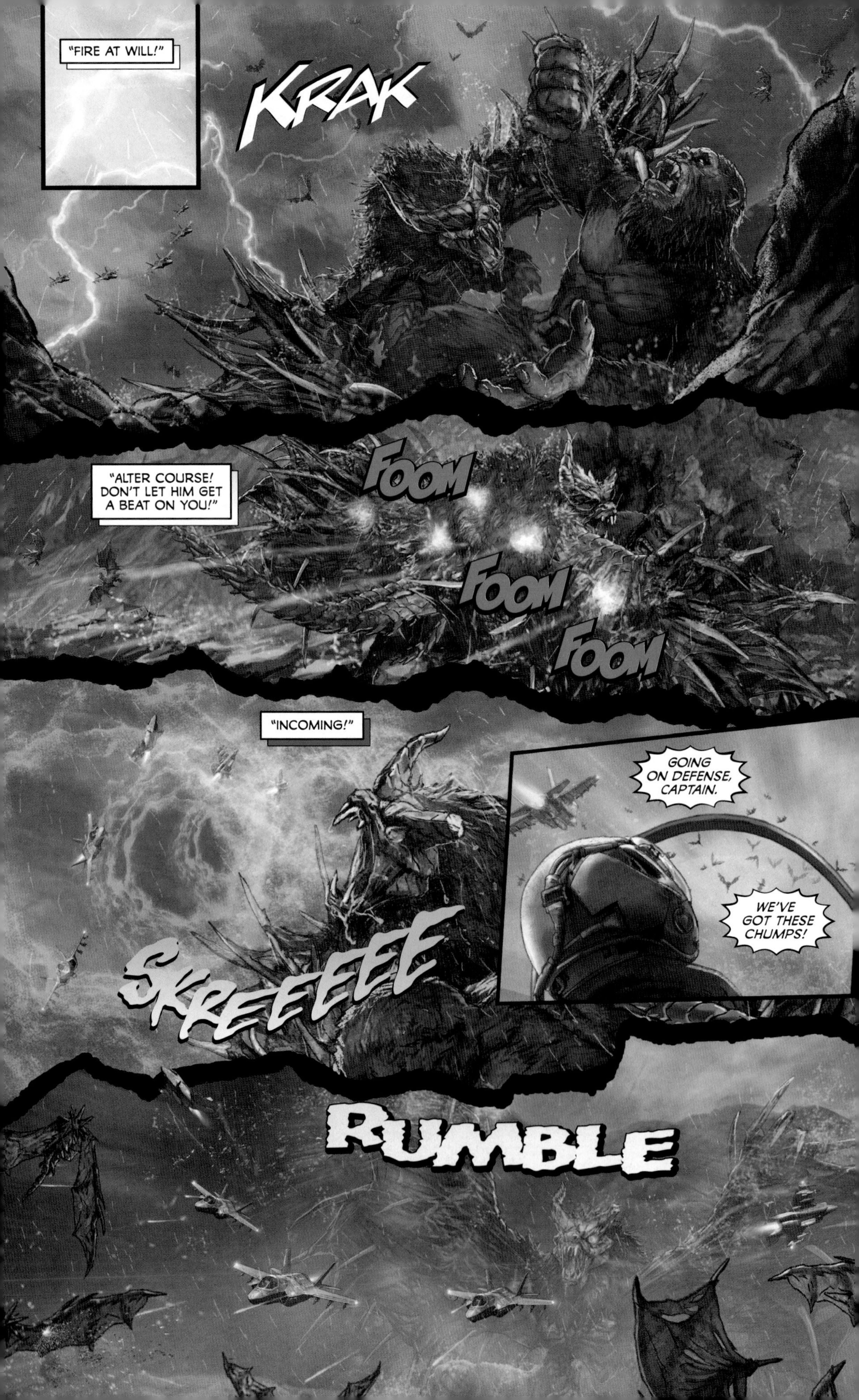
"FIRE AT WILL!"
KRAK
"ALTER COURSE! DON'T LET HIM GET A BEAT ON YOU!"
FOOM
FOOM
FOOM
"INCOMING!"
GOING ON DEFENSE, CAPTAIN.
WE'VE GOT THESE CHUMPS!
SKREEEEEE
RUMBLE

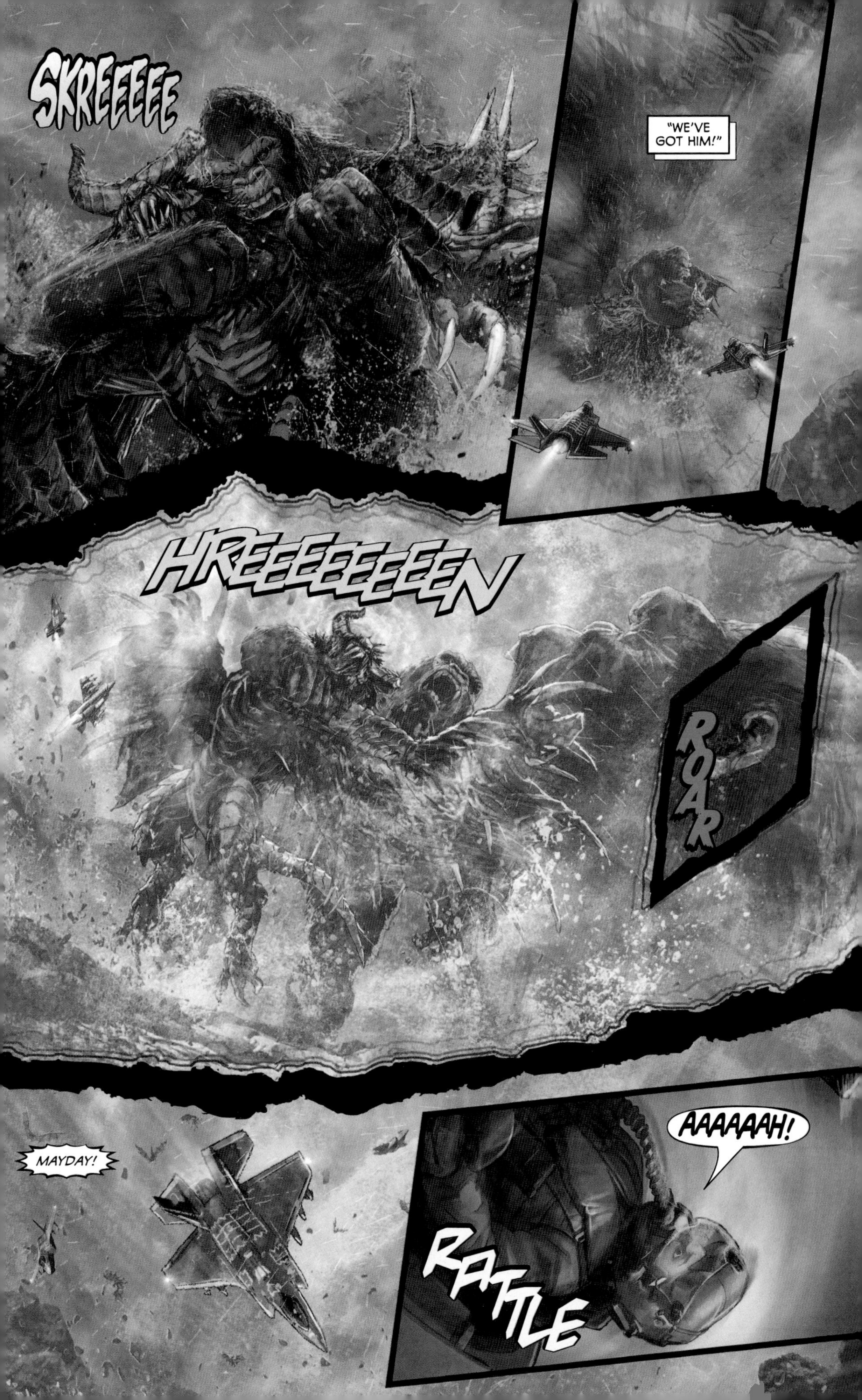
SKREEEEEE
"WE'VE GOT HIM!"
HREEEEEEEEEN
ROAR
MAYDAY!
AAAAAAH!
RATTLE

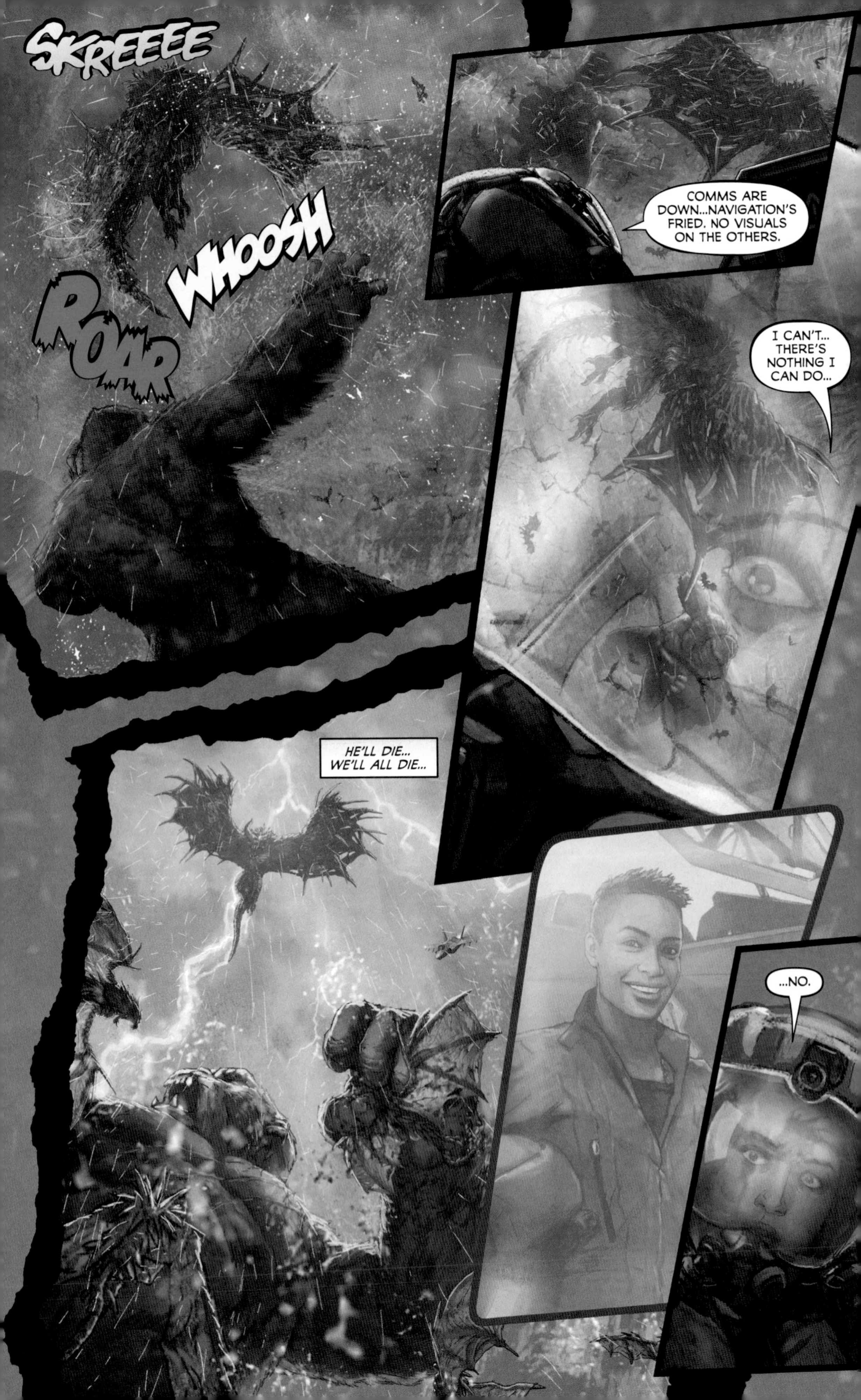
SKREEEE
WHOOSH
ROAR
COMMS ARE DOWN...NAVIGATION'S FRIED. NO VISUALS ON THE OTHERS.
I CAN'T... THERE'S NOTHING I CAN DO...
HE'LL DIE... WE'LL ALL DIE...
...NO.

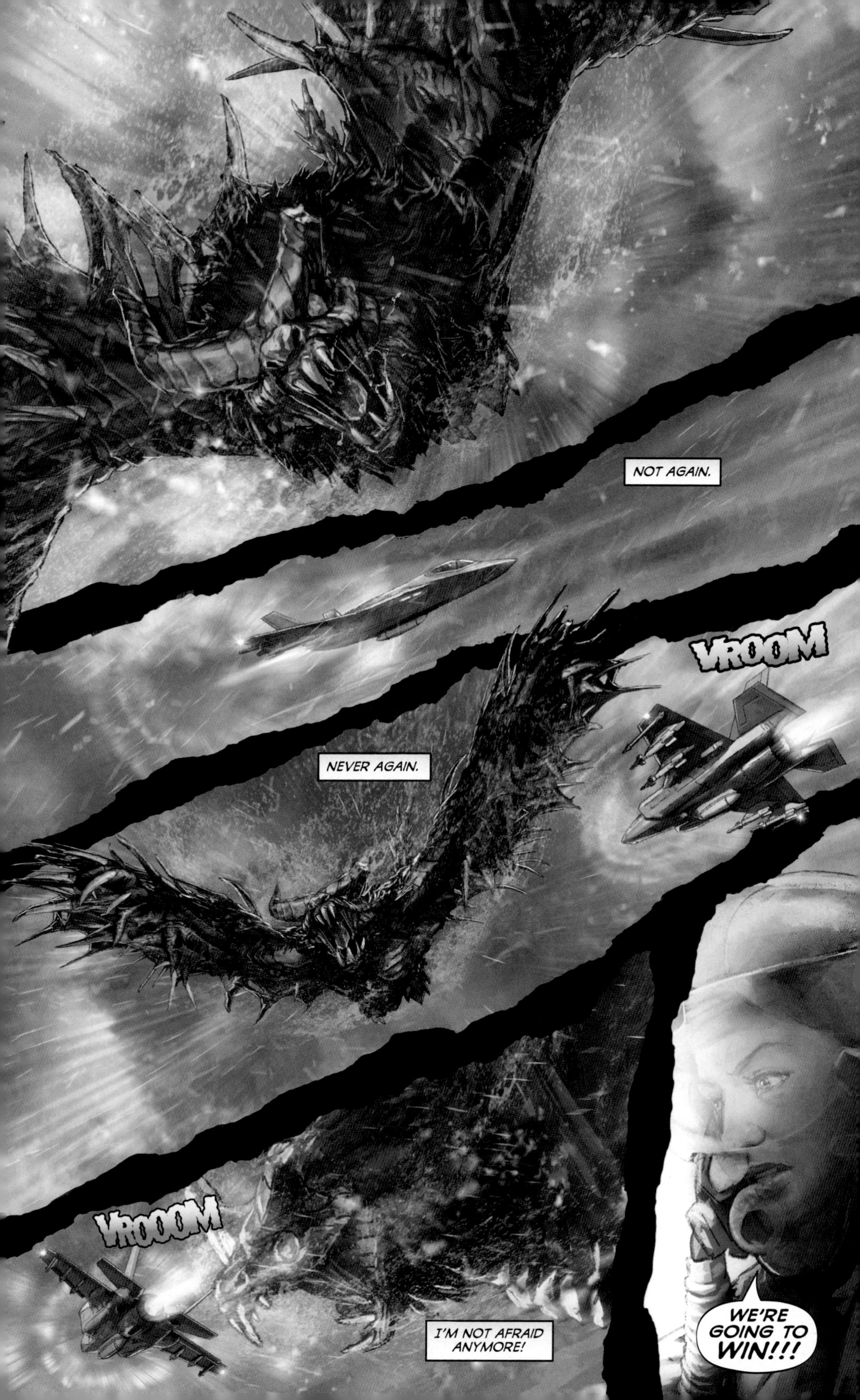
NOT AGAIN.
VROOM
NEVER AGAIN.
VROOOM
I'M NOT AFRAID ANYMORE!
WE'RE GOING TO WIN!!!

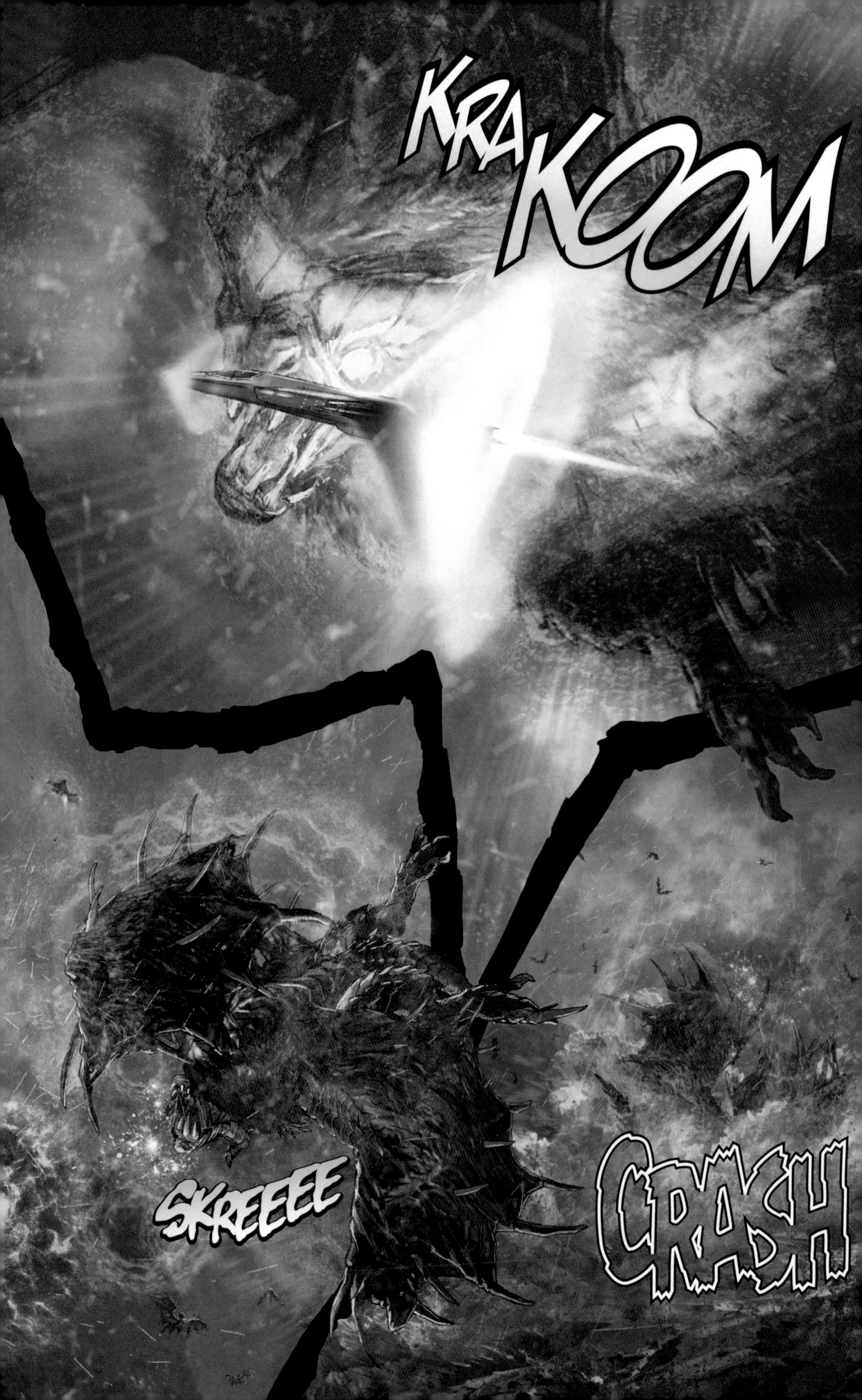
KRA
KOOOM
SKREEEE
CRASH

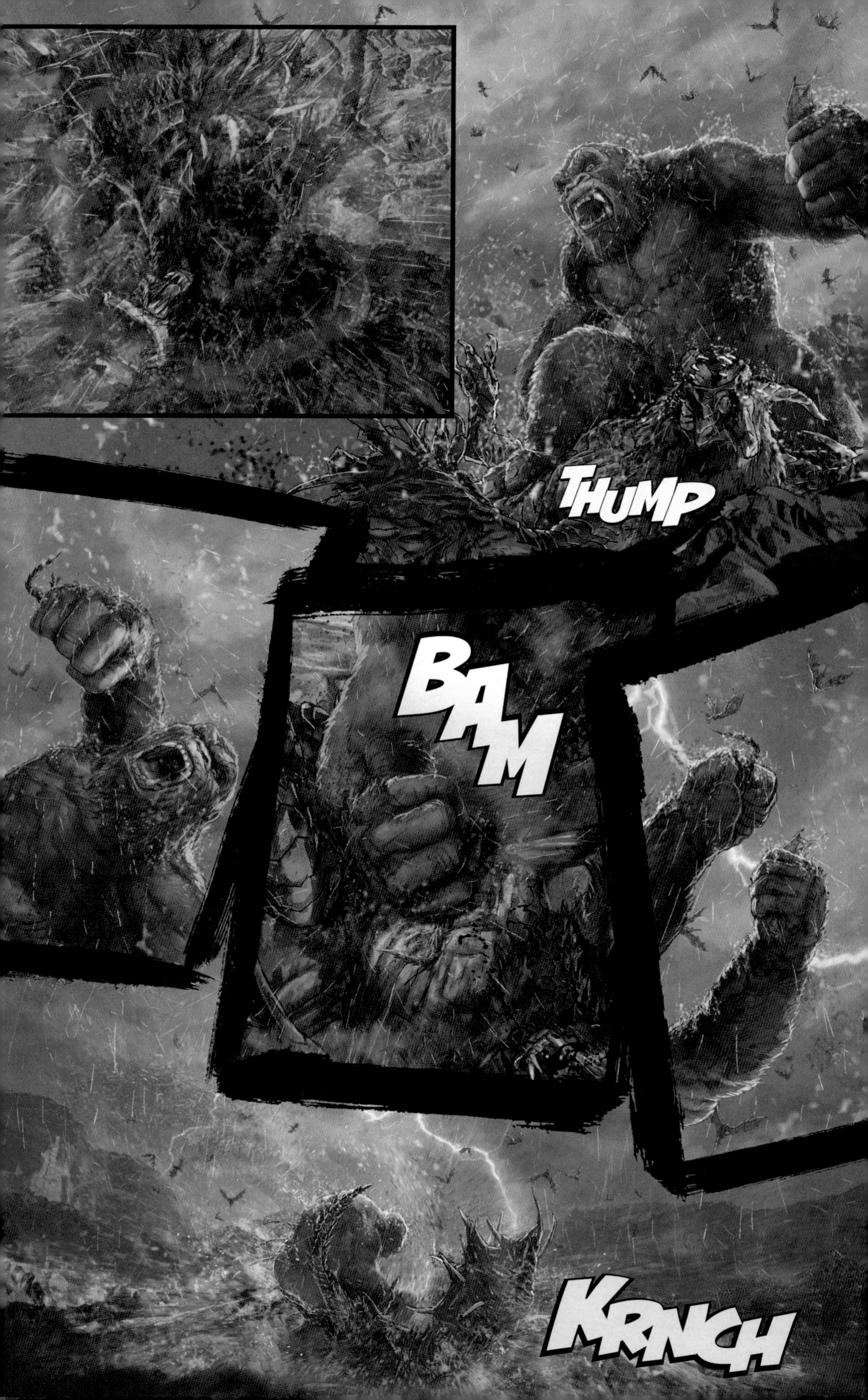
THUMP
BAM
KRNCH

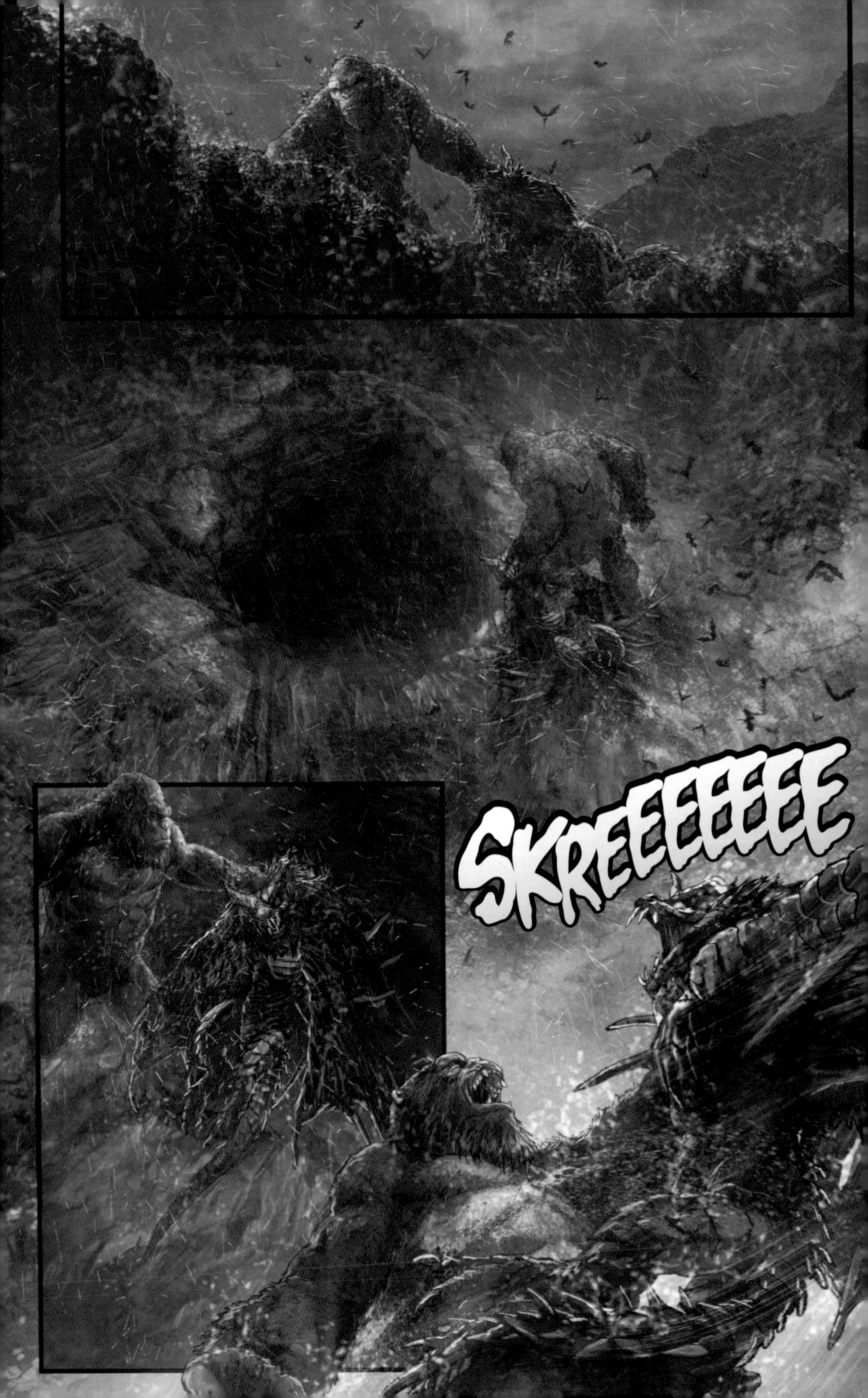
SKREEEEEEEE

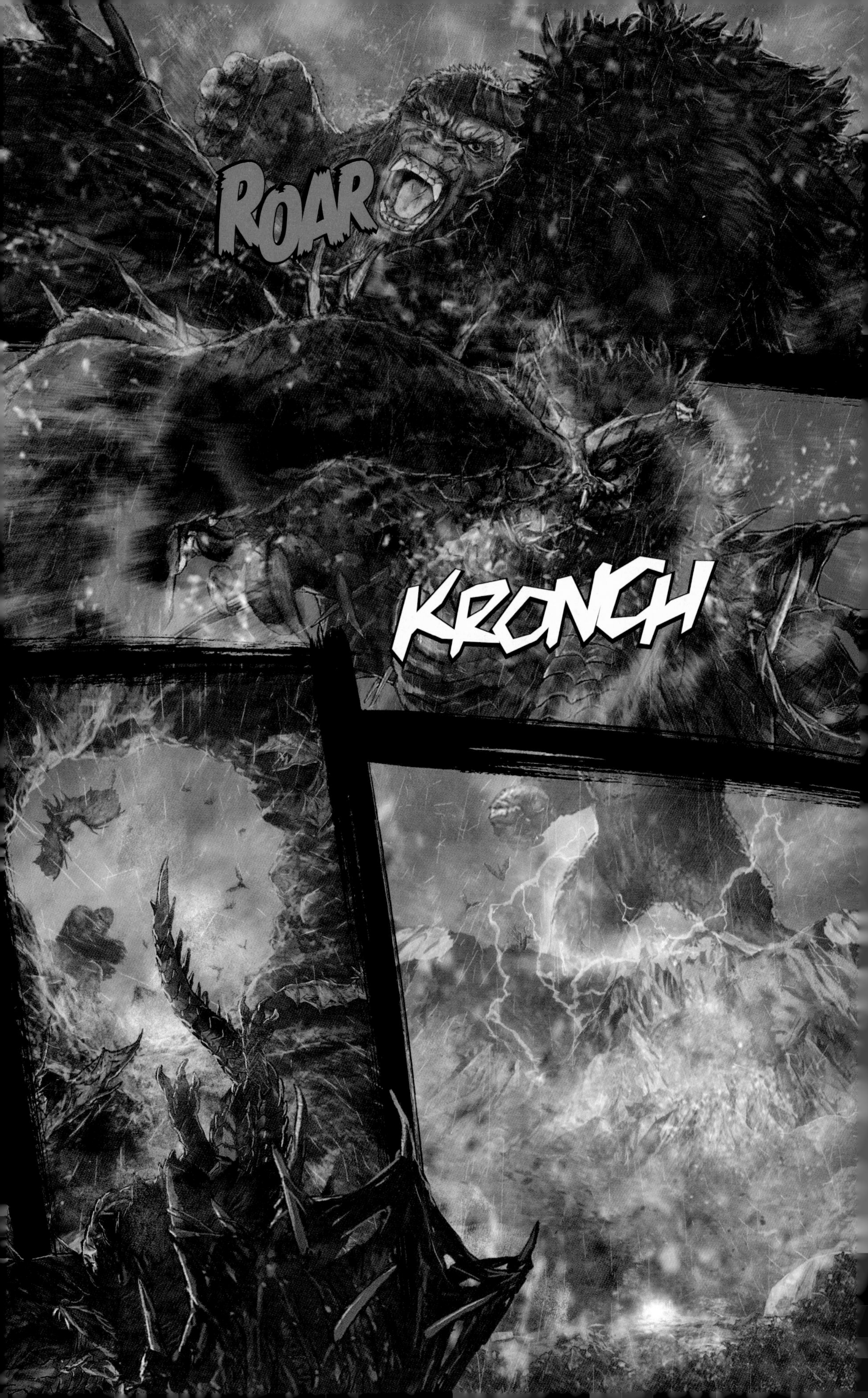
ROAR
KRONCH

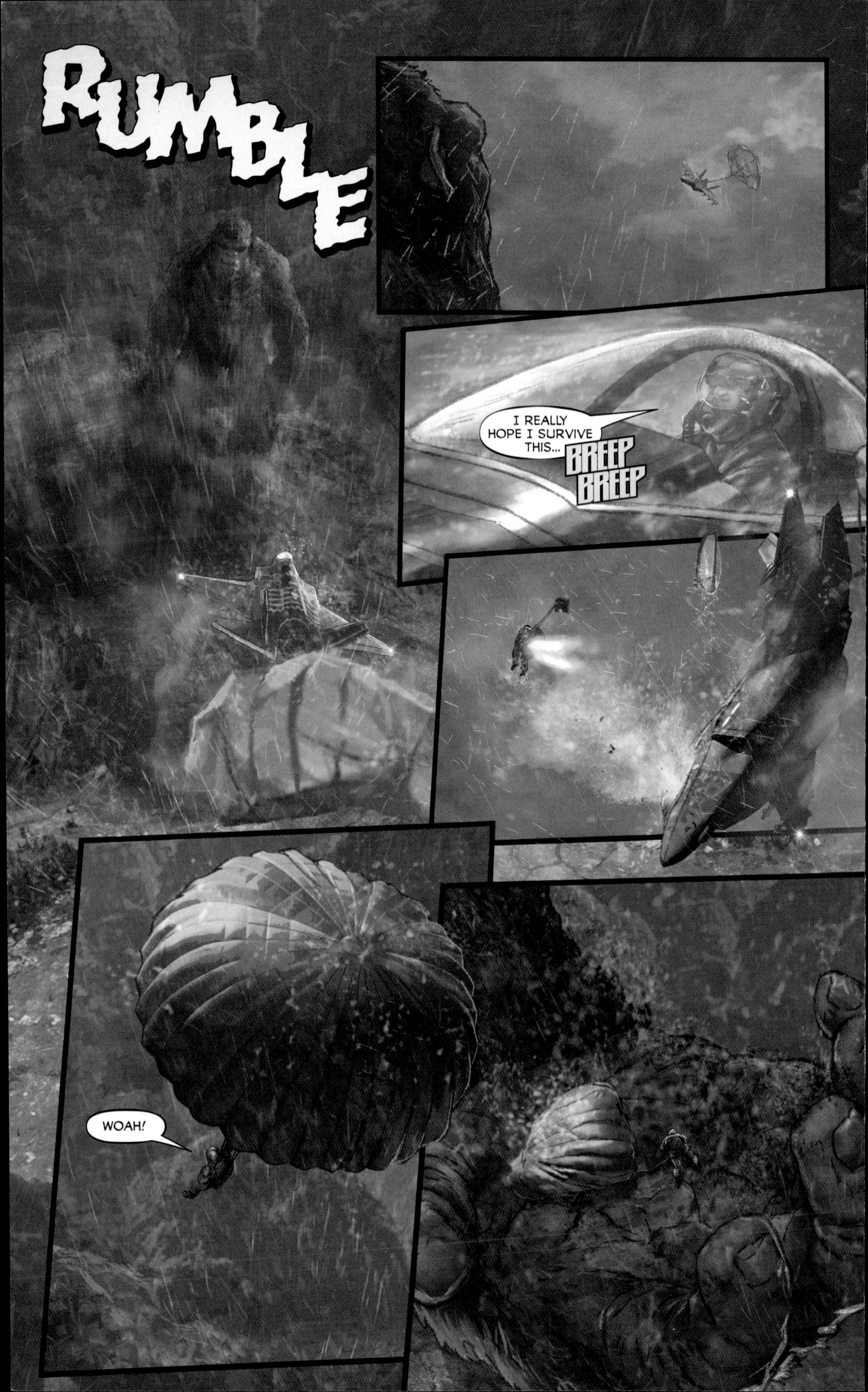
RUMBLE
I REALLY HOPE I SURVIVE THIS...
BREEP BREEP
WOAH!

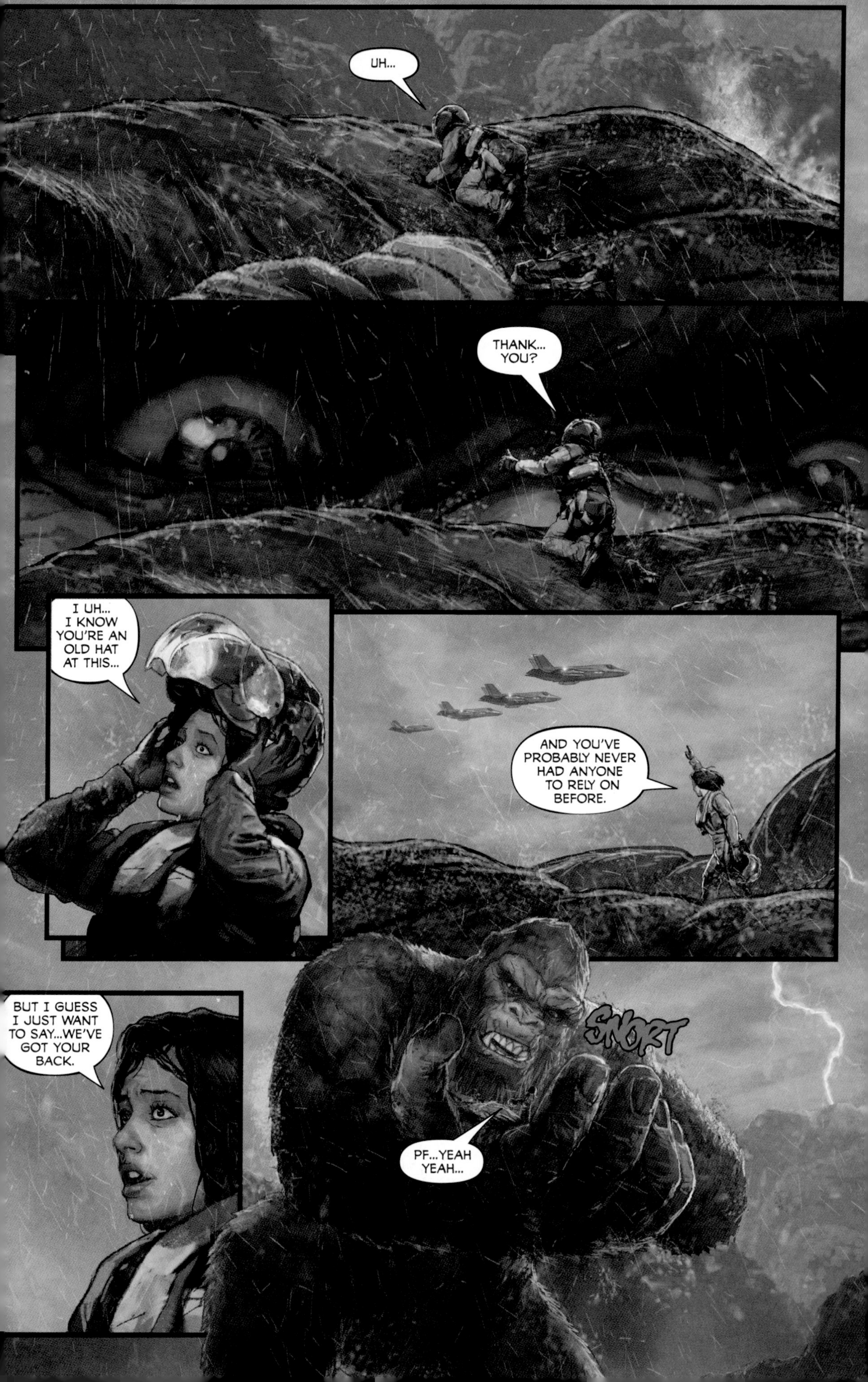
UH...
THANK... YOU?
I UH... I KNOW YOU'RE AN OLD HAT AT THIS...
AND YOU'VE PROBABLY NEVER HAD ANYONE TO RELY ON BEFORE.
BUT I GUESS I JUST WANT TO SAY...WE'VE GOT YOUR BACK.
SNORT
PF...YEAH YEAH...

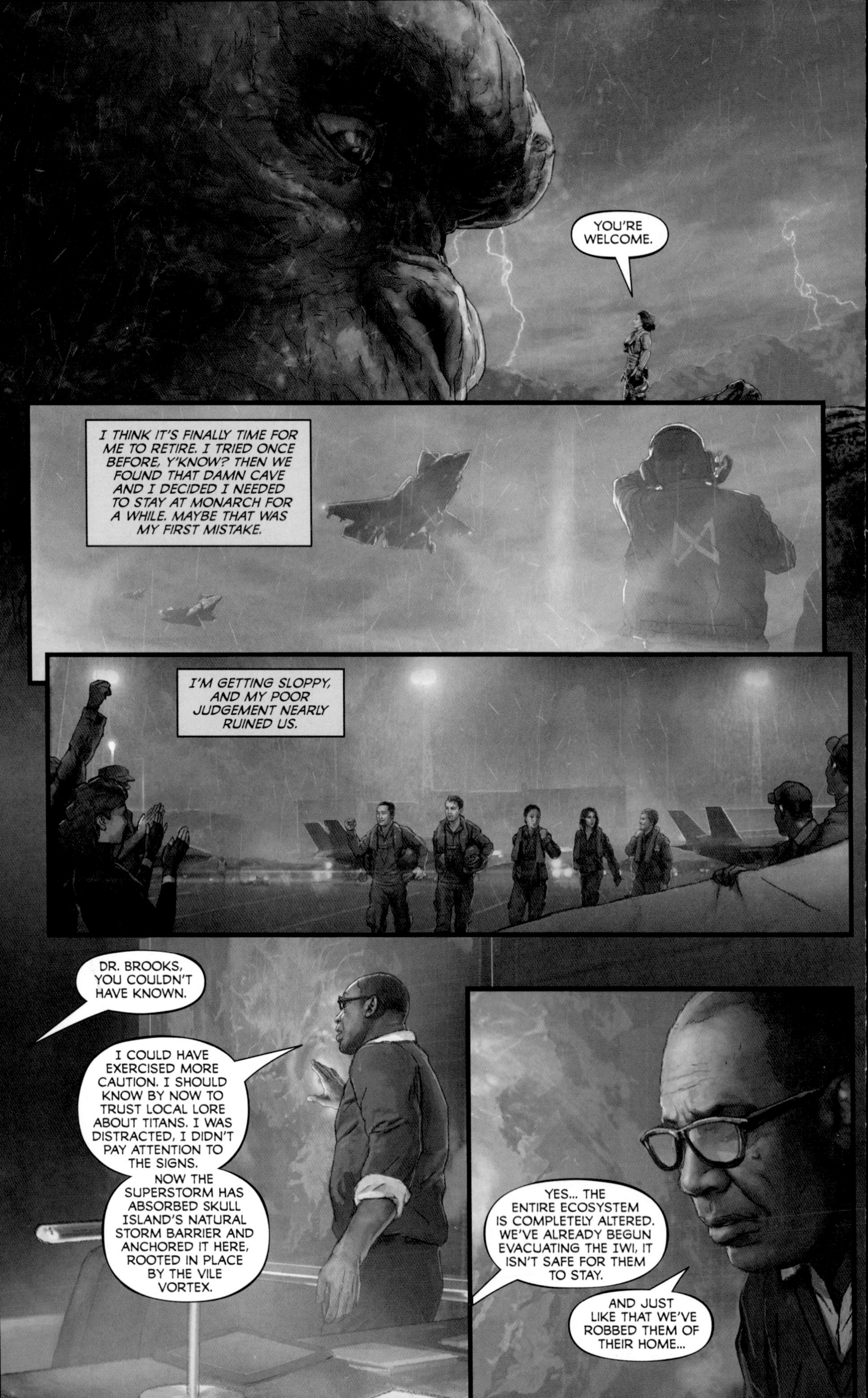

YOU'RE WELCOME.
I THINK IT'S FINALLY TIME FOR ME TO RETIRE. I TRIED ONCE BEFORE, Y'KNOW? THEN WE FOUND THAT DAMN CAVE AND I DECIDED I NEEDED TO STAY AT MONARCH FOR A WHILE. MAYBE THAT WAS MY FIRST MISTAKE.
I'M GETTING SLOPPY, AND MY POOR JUDGEMENT NEARLY RUINED US.
DR. BROOKS, YOU COULDN'T HAVE KNOWN.
I COULD HAVE EXERCISED MORE CAUTION. I SHOULD KNOW BY NOW TO TRUST LOCAL LORE ABOUT TITANS. I WAS DISTRACTED, I DIDN'T PAY ATTENTION TO THE SIGNS.
NOW THE SUPERSTORM HAS ABSORBED SKULL ISLAND'S NATURAL STORM BARRIER AND ANCHORED IT HERE, ROOTED IN PLACE BY THE VILE VORTEX.
YES... THE ENTIRE ECOSYSTEM IS COMPLETELY ALTERED. WE'VE ALREADY BEGUN EVACUATING THE IWI, IT ISN'T SAFE FOR THEM TO STAY.
AND JUST LIKE THAT WE'VE ROBBED THEM OF THEIR HOME...

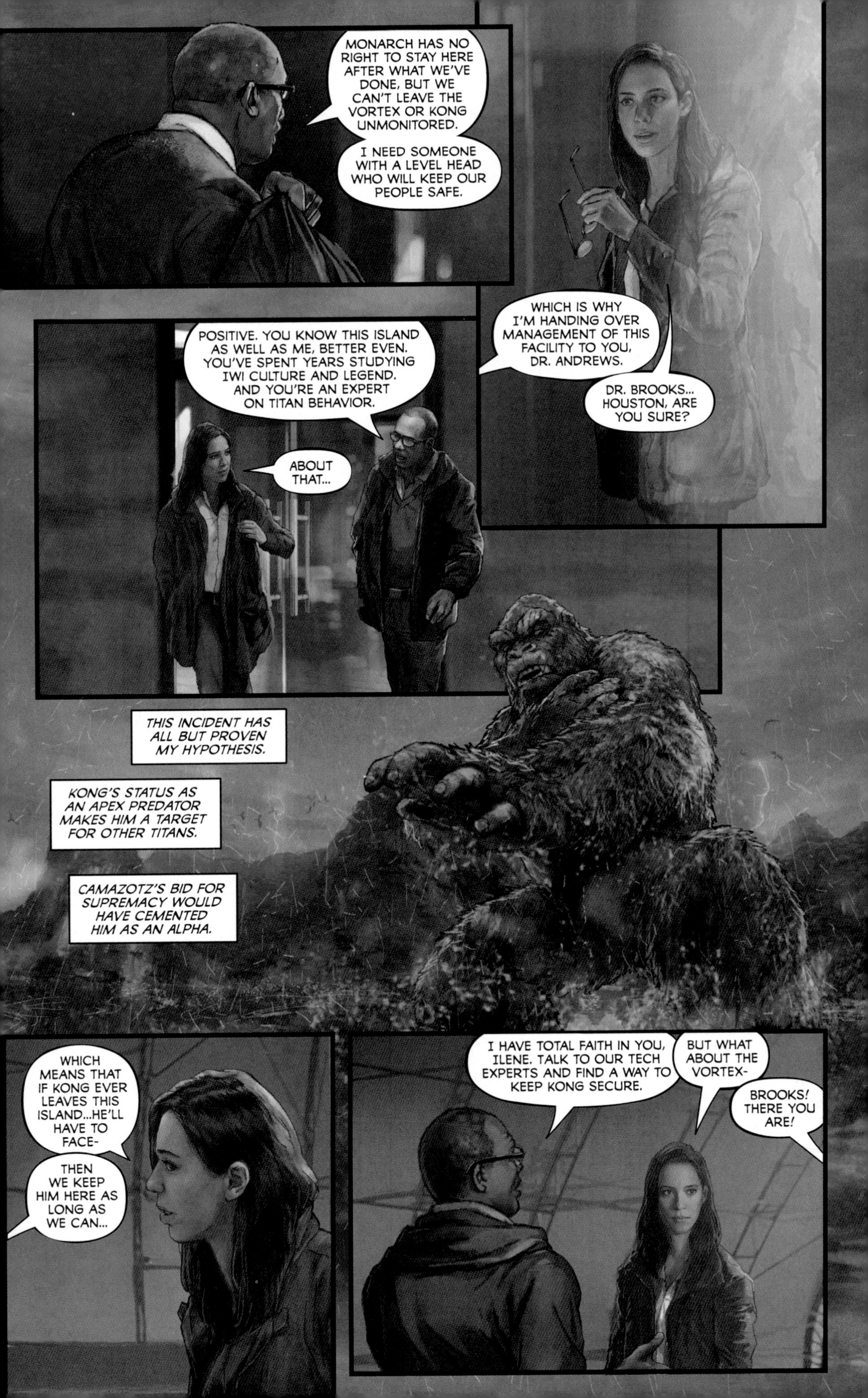
MONARCH HAS NO RIGHT TO STAY HERE AFTER WHAT WE'VE DONE, BUT WE CAN'T LEAVE THE VORTEX OR KONG UNMONITORED.
I NEED SOMEONE WITH A LEVEL HEAD WHO WILL KEEP OUR PEOPLE SAFE.
WHICH IS WHY I'M HANDING OVER MANAGEMENT OF THIS FACILITY TO YOU, DR. ANDREWS.
DR. BROOKS... HOUSTON, ARE YOU SURE?
POSITIVE. YOU KNOW THIS ISLAND AS WELL AS ME, BETTER EVEN. YOU'VE SPENT YEARS STUDYING IWI CULTURE AND LEGEND. AND YOU'RE AN EXPERT ON TITAN BEHAVIOR.
ABOUT THAT...
THIS INCIDENT HAS ALL BUT PROVEN MY HYPOTHESIS.
KONG'S STATUS AS AN APEX PREDATOR MAKES HIM A TARGET FOR OTHER TITANS.
CAMAZOTZ'S BID FOR SUPREMACY WOULD HAVE CEMENTED HIM AS AN ALPHA.
WHICH MEANS THAT IF KONG EVER LEAVES THIS ISLAND...HE'LL HAVE TO FACE-
THEN WE KEEP HIM HERE AS LONG AS WE CAN...
I HAVE TOTAL FAITH IN YOU, ILENE. TALK TO OUR TECH EXPERTS AND FIND A WAY TO KEEP KONG SECURE.
BUT WHAT ABOUT THE VORTEX-
BROOKS! THERE YOU ARE!

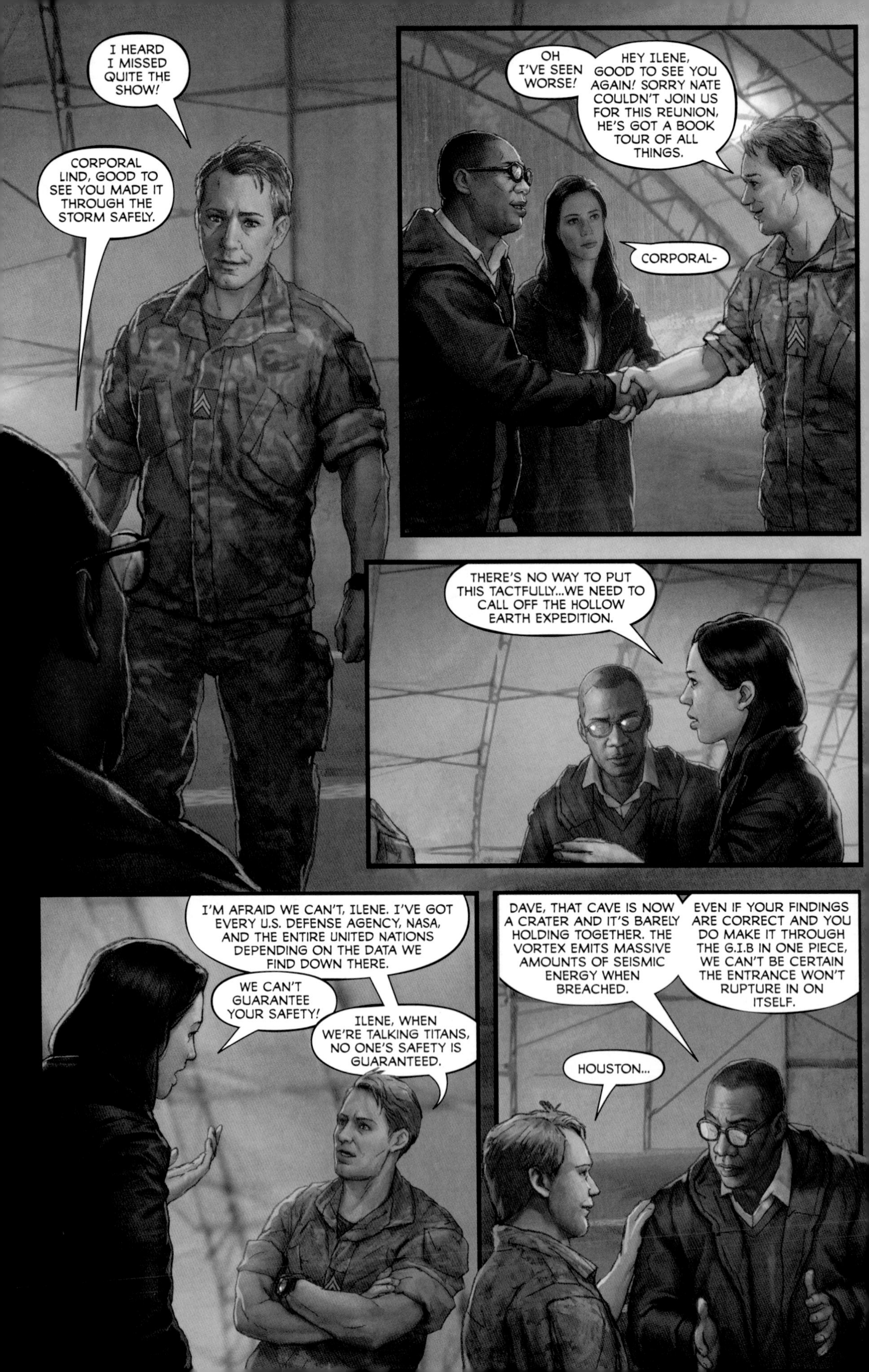
I HEARD I MISSED QUITE THE SHOW!
CORPORAL LIND, GOOD TO SEE YOU MADE IT THROUGH THE STORM SAFELY.
OH I'VE SEEN WORSE!
HEY ILENE, GOOD TO SEE YOU AGAIN! SORRY NATE COULDN'T JOIN US FOR THIS REUNION, HE'S GOT A BOOK TOUR OF ALL THINGS.
CORPORAL-
THERE'S NO WAY TO PUT THIS TACTFULLY...WE NEED TO CALL OFF THE HOLLOW EARTH EXPEDITION.
I'M AFRAID WE CAN'T, ILENE. I'VE GOT EVERY U.S. DEFENSE AGENCY, NASA, AND THE ENTIRE UNITED NATIONS DEPENDING ON THE DATA WE FIND DOWN THERE.
WE CAN'T GUARANTEE YOUR SAFETY!
ILENE, WHEN WE'RE TALKING TITANS, NO ONE'S SAFETY IS GUARANTEED.
DAVE, THAT CAVE IS NOW A CRATER AND IT'S BARELY HOLDING TOGETHER. THE VORTEX EMITS MASSIVE AMOUNTS OF SEISMIC ENERGY WHEN BREACHED.
EVEN IF YOUR FINDINGS ARE CORRECT AND YOU DO MAKE IT THROUGH THE G.I.B IN ONE PIECE, WE CAN'T BE CERTAIN THE ENTRANCE WON'T RUPTURE IN ON ITSELF.
HOUSTON...

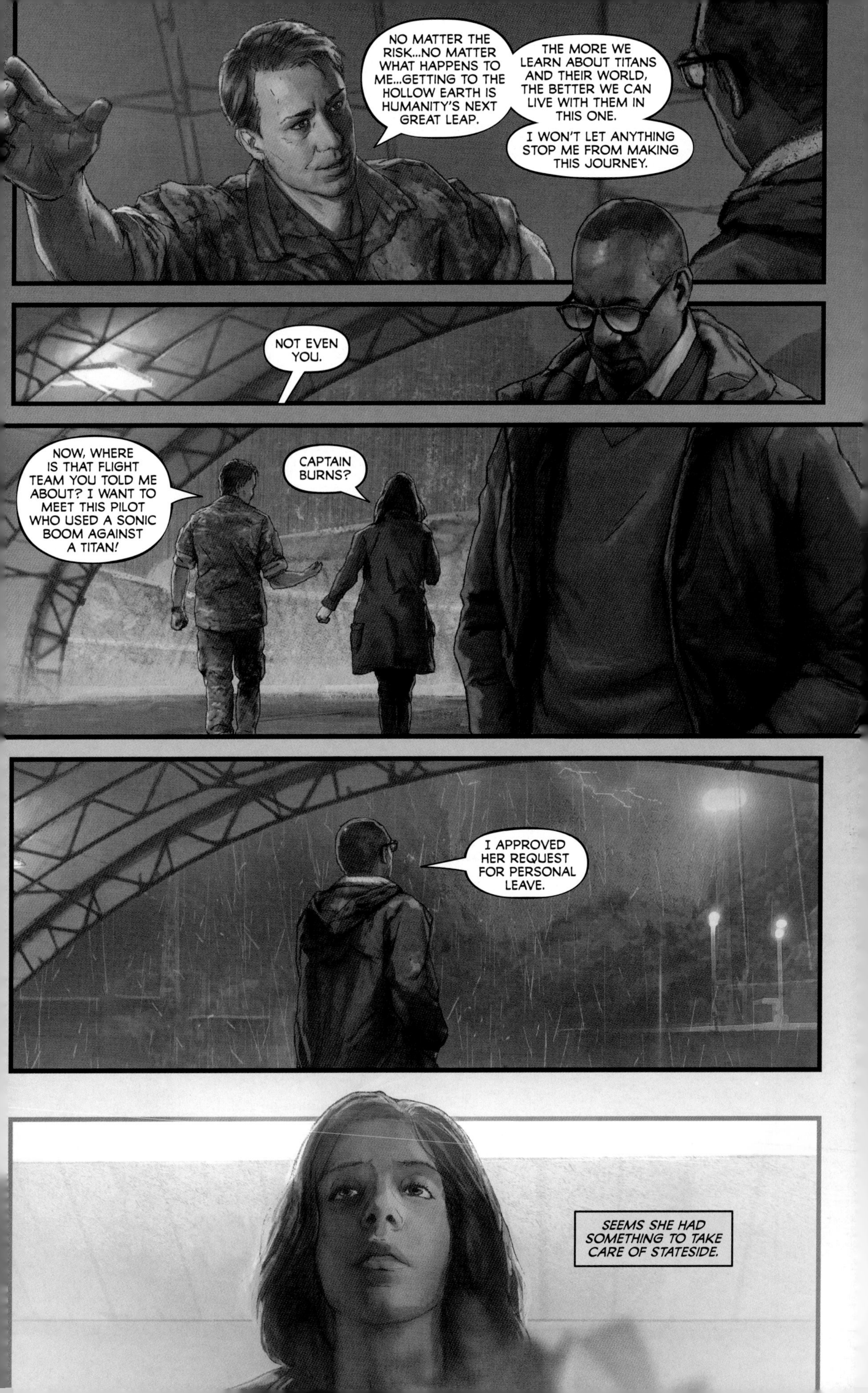
NO MATTER THE RISK...NO MATTER WHAT HAPPENS TO ME...GETTING TO THE HOLLOW EARTH IS HUMANITY'S NEXT GREAT LEAP.
THE MORE WE LEARN ABOUT TITANS AND THEIR WORLD, THE BETTER WE CAN LIVE WITH THEM IN THIS ONE.
I WON'T LET ANYTHING STOP ME FROM MAKING THIS JOURNEY.
NOT EVEN YOU.
NOW, WHERE IS THAT FLIGHT TEAM YOU TOLD ME ABOUT? I WANT TO MEET THIS PILOT WHO USED A SONIC BOOM AGAINST A TITAN!
CAPTAIN BURNS?
I APPROVED HER REQUEST FOR PERSONAL LEAVE.
SEEMS SHE HAD SOMETHING TO TAKE CARE OF STATESIDE.

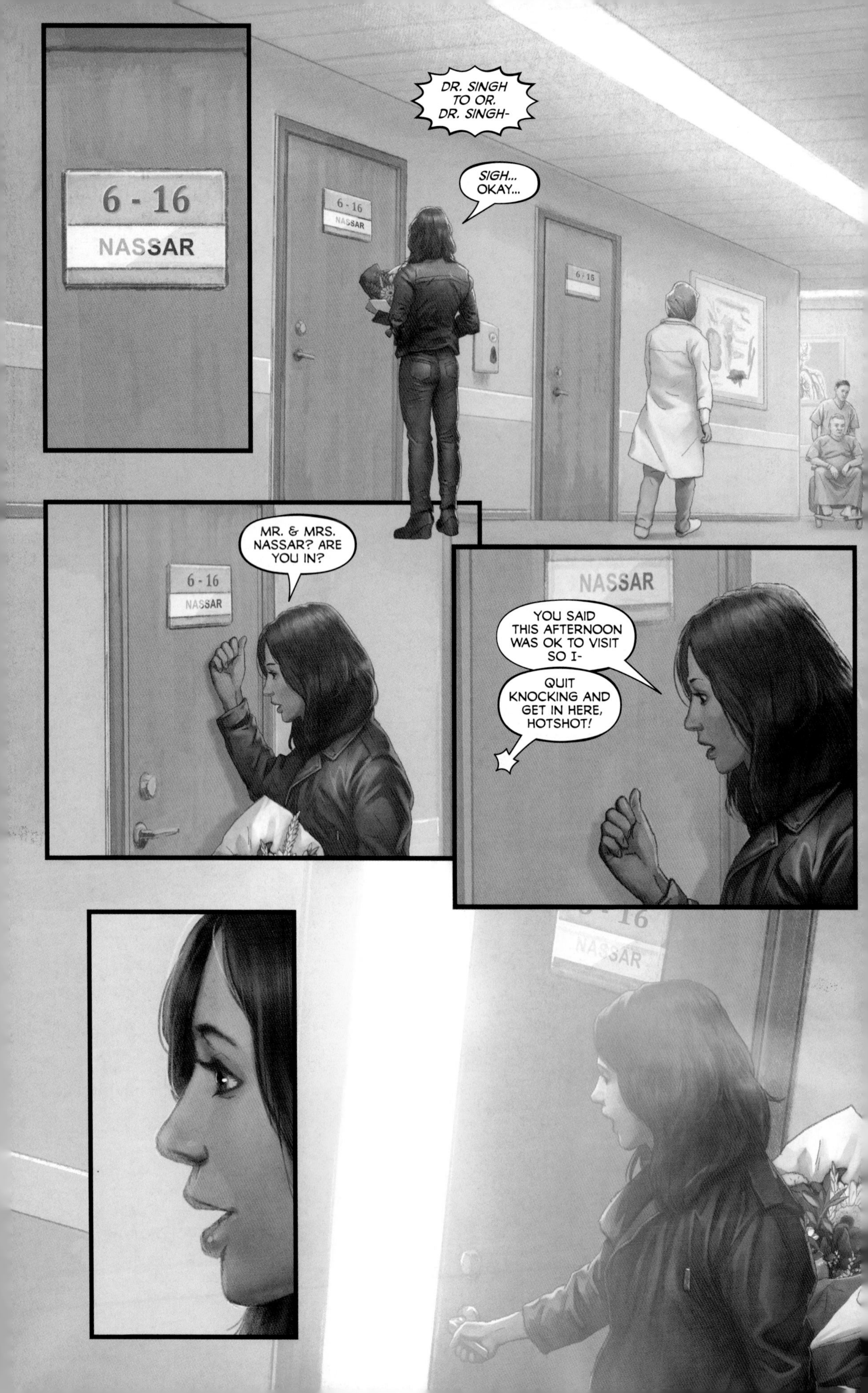
6 - 16
NASSAR
DR. SINGH TO OR. DR. SINGH-
SIGH... OKAY...
MR. & MRS. NASSAR? ARE YOU IN?
YOU SAID THIS AFTERNOON WAS OK TO VISIT SO I-
QUIT KNOCKING AND GET IN HERE, HOTSHOT!

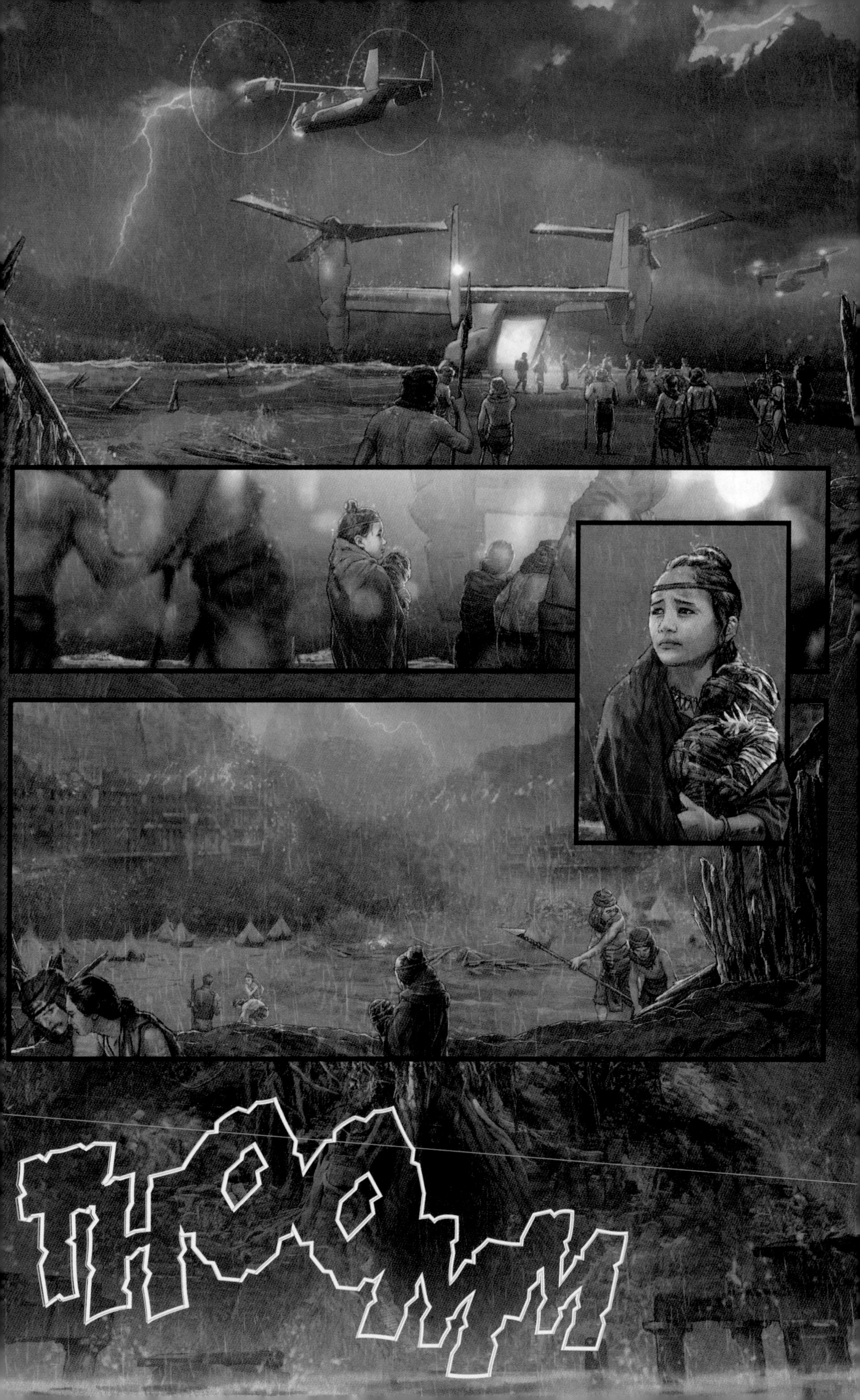
THOOMM

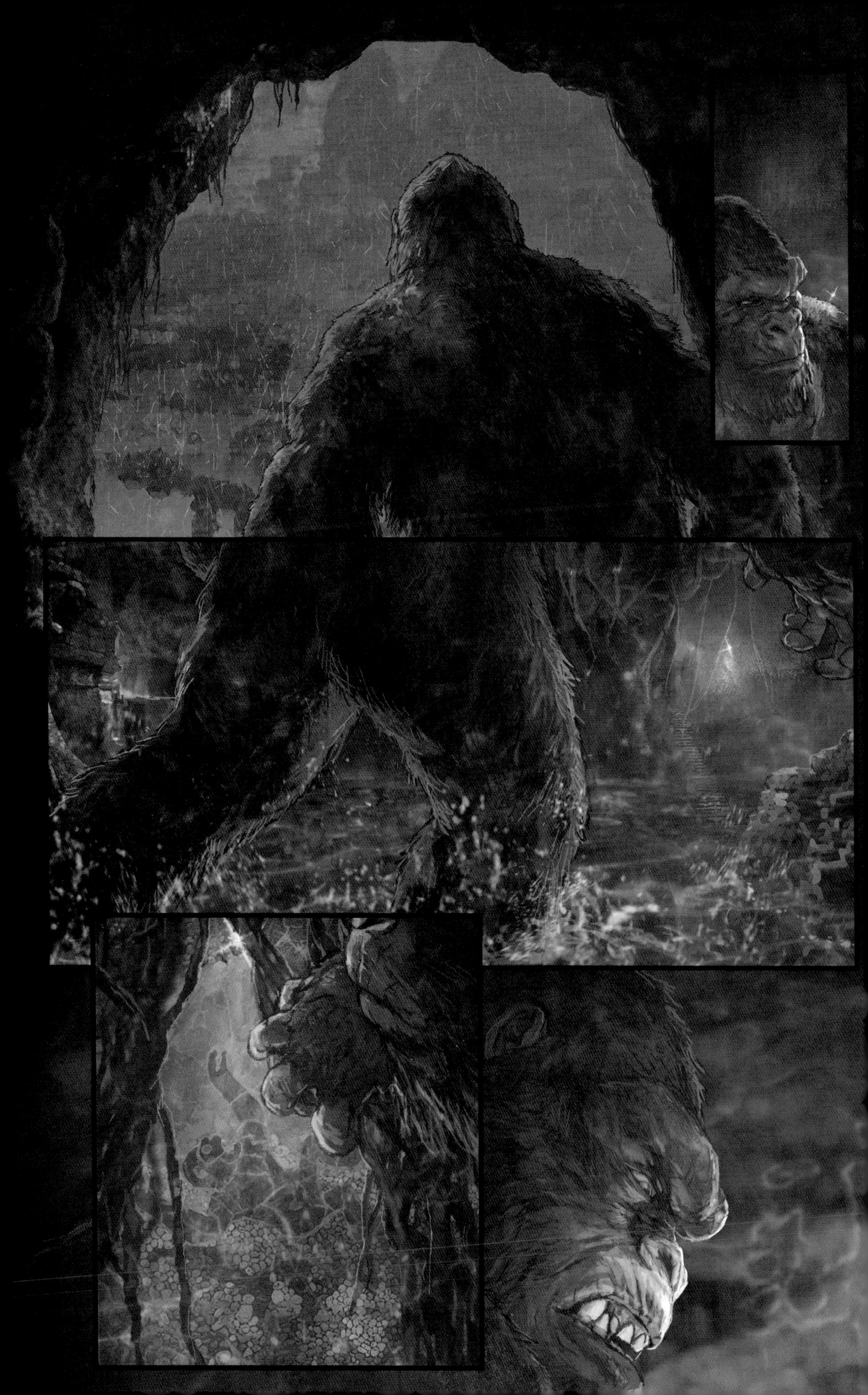

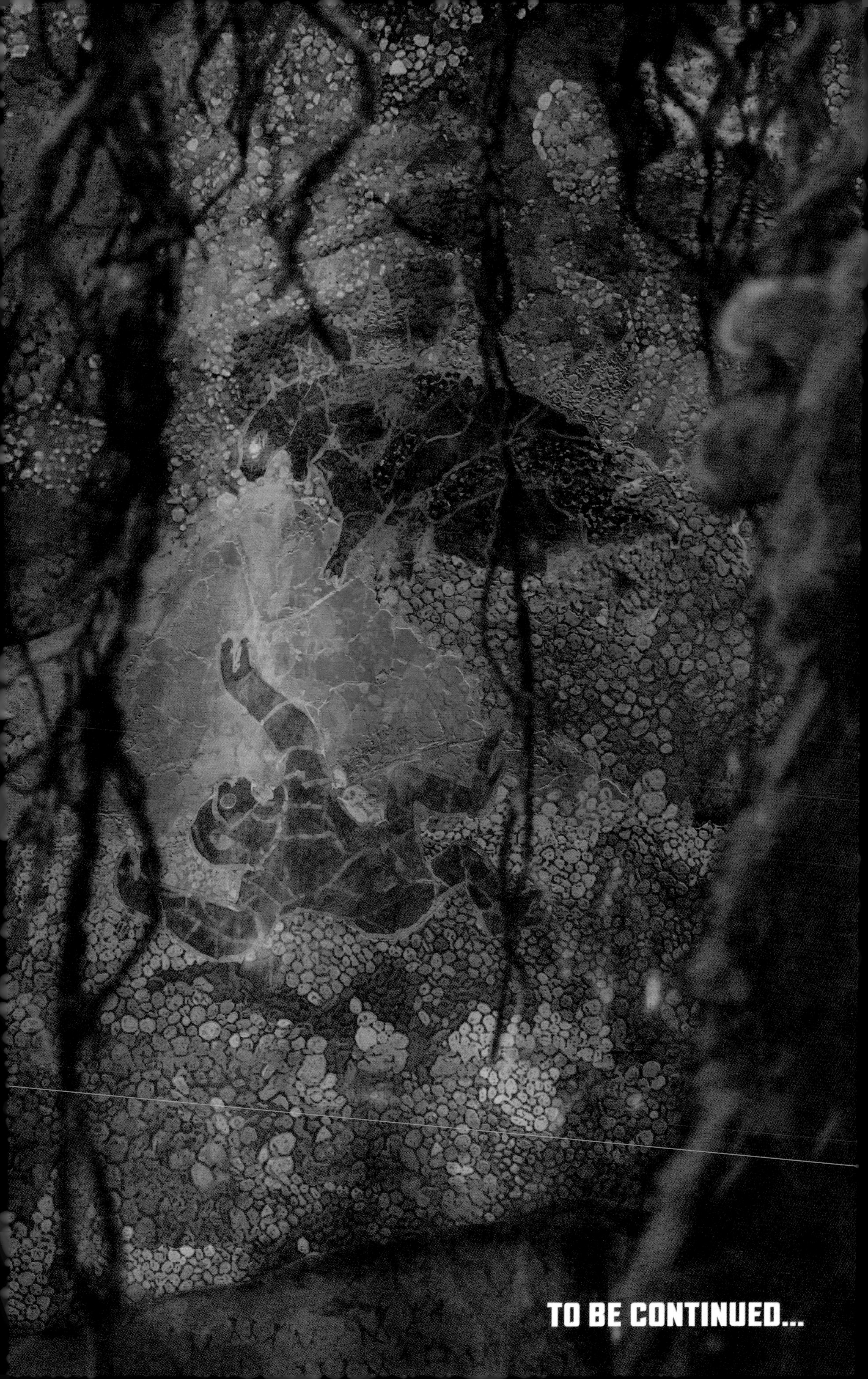
TO BE CONTINUED...

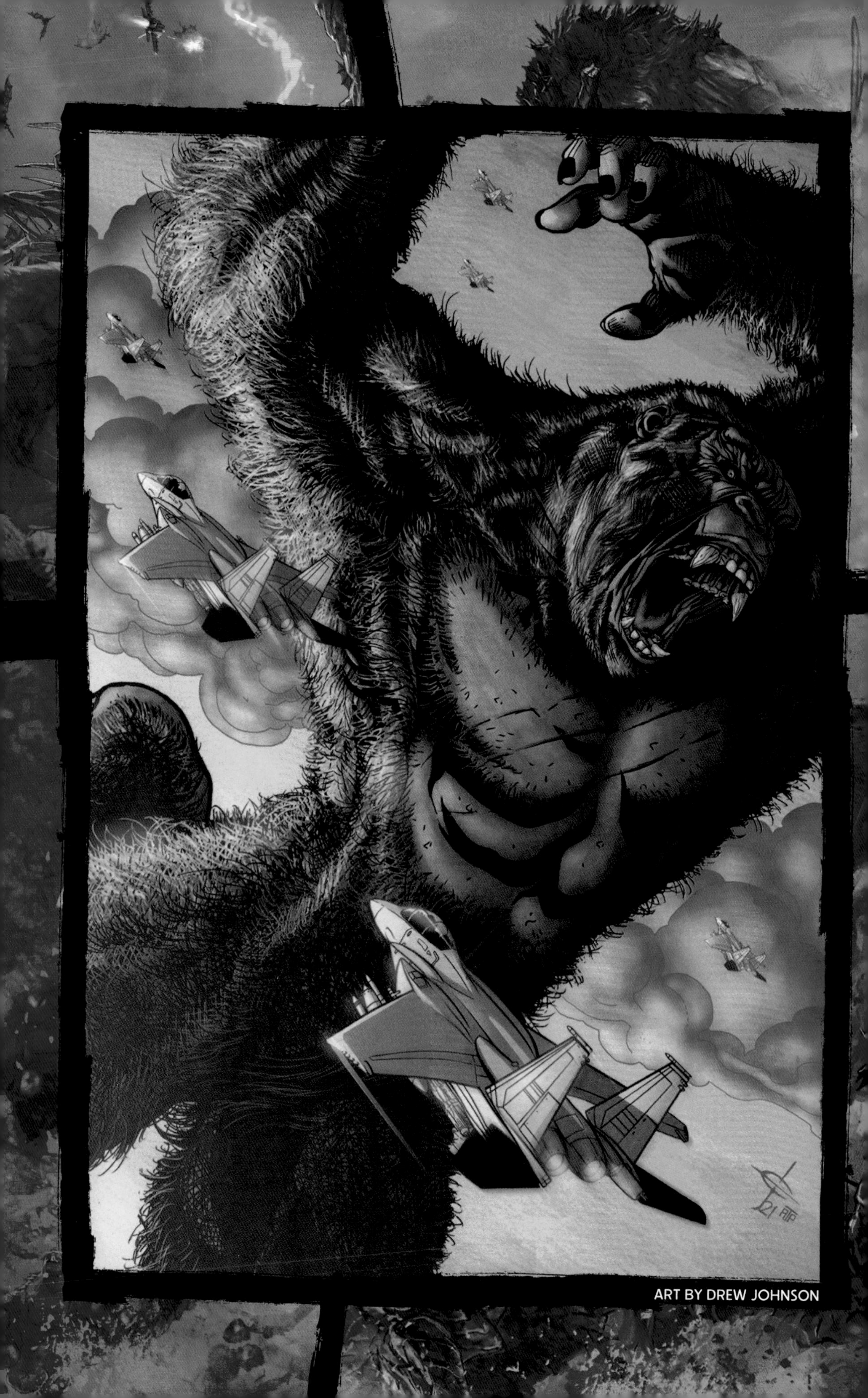

ART BY DREW JOHNSON

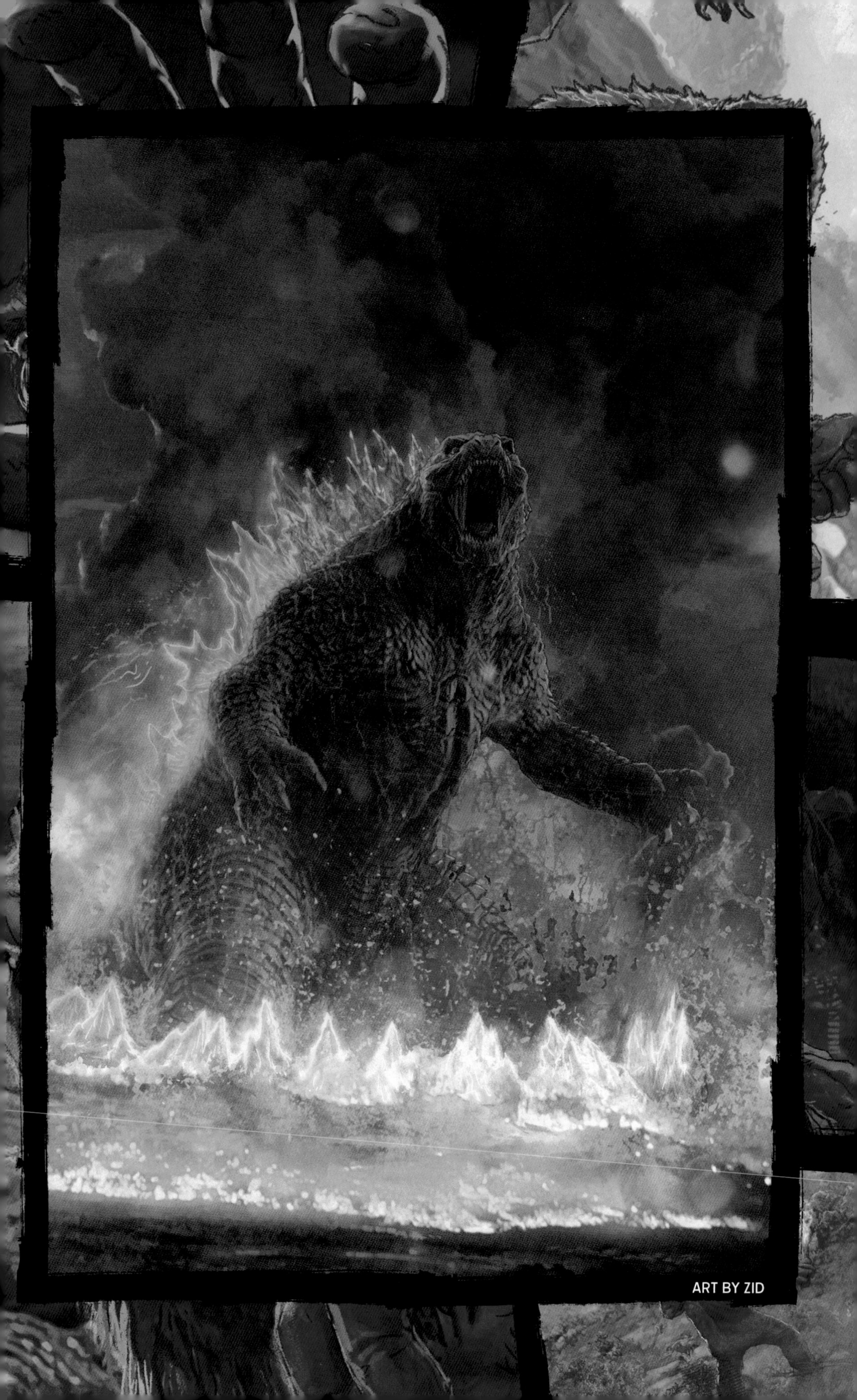

ART BY ZID

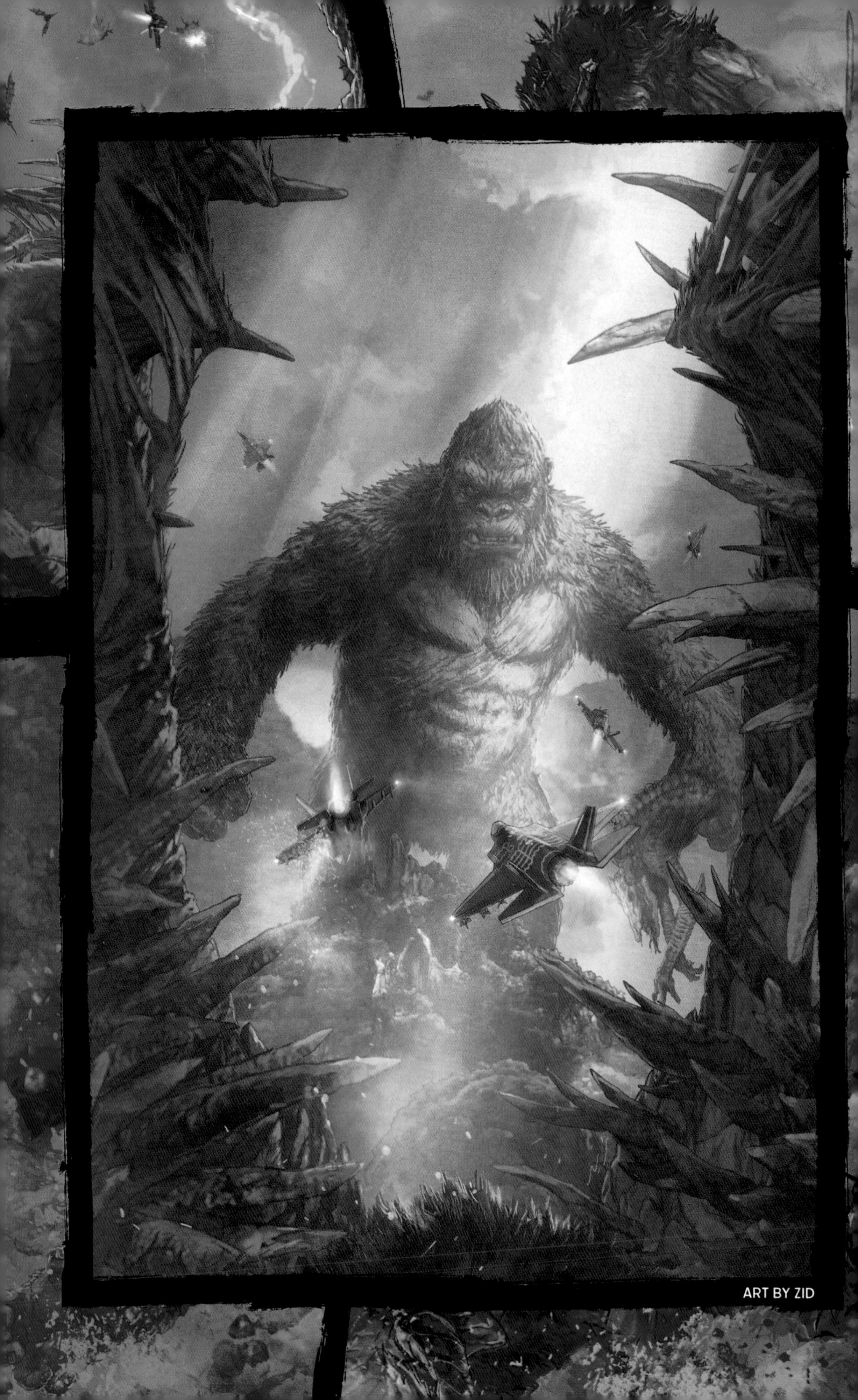

ART BY ZID

2 | COM.SYS 0067 | 0850 | CONNECT | 0017-32A | CONNECTION:L | DATALINK:12 | bot G:MASTER [C/1H

NECT> | bot G:MASTER [C/1H abbrev] – 17:20 ——— | PERIMETER SURV.

MONARCH

OL

PWR TMP CMS

VIEW REPORTS

DSP CRNT
ACTIVE

HOST IP
10.0.92.256

MN.RESEND | ELIP | CONNECTION:L DTLINK | 75.5 | COMS.SYS - REF DB

LINK VER CODE LIN1 LIN2 SEC DATA MODE CONNECTION:L DATALINK:12 COM.SYS 0067 0850

NET.IO USR: <UNKNOWN> -UU- :@ — F4 admin.h NET.IO USR: <CONNECT> bot G:MASTER [C/1H

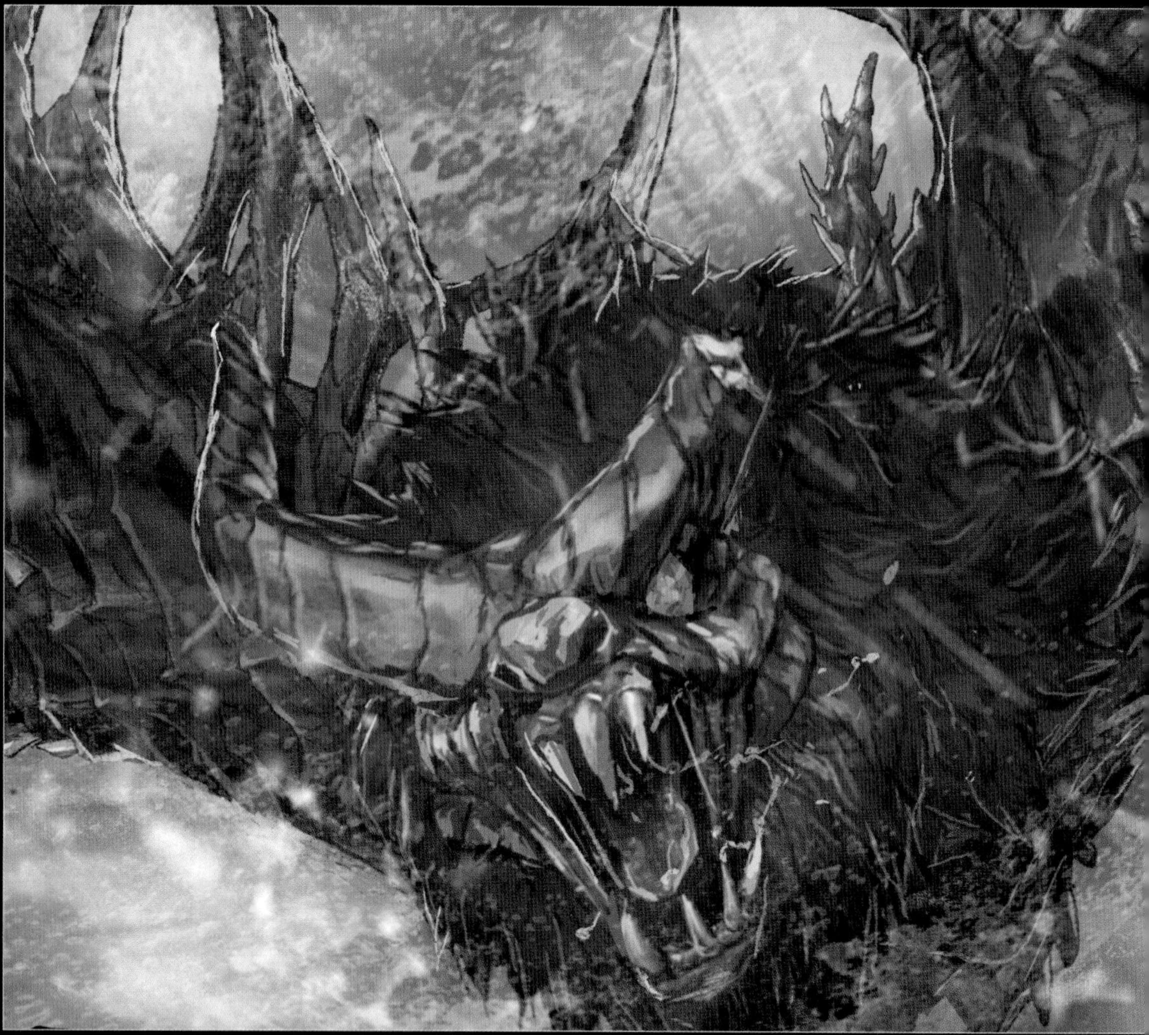

SUPERSPECIES STATISTICS

MONARCH DESIGNATION: **CAMAZOTZ**

CLASSIFICATION: **TITANUS CAMAZOTZ**

NATURE: **BIO-SONIC**

BODY HEIGHT: **164 FEET**

WINGSPAN: **402 FEET**

BEHAVIOR **DESTROYER**

RANGE: **WORLDWIDE**

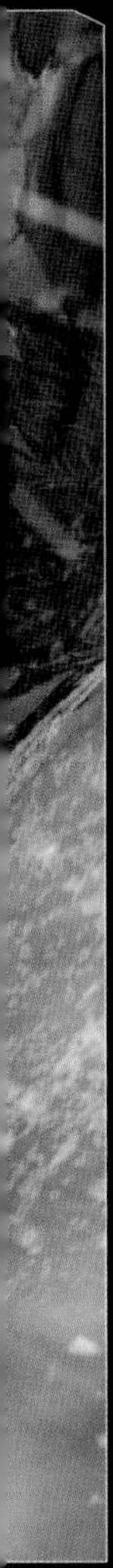

CREATURE PROFILE

THE MYTH

A cult following for the creature began amongst the Zapotec Indians of Oaxaca, Mexico, and the figure was later adopted into the pantheon of the Maya Quiche tribe. The legends of the bat god were later recorded in Maya literature. The cult believed bats represented night, death, and sacrifice, likely due to the fact that the bats would inhabit the caves around the sacred cenotes, which the Mesoamericans believed were portals to the underworld.

THE REALITY

Carved in stone by the fearful hands of ancient Mayans as a warning for the future to discover, the myth of the dark Titan Camazotz is a nightmarish reality that has cursed the skies of humanity since the dawn of time. Blinded from dwelling for millennia in the deepest and darkest caverns of the Hollow Earth, Camazotz is guided by echolocation and a ravenous thirst for atomic-rich Titan blood. Its sonic screech can shatter entire buildings and disrupt the senses of opposing Titans in combat. With its ancient name translating to "Death Bat", Camazotz flies on torn leather wings jutting with razorblades of jagged bone, controlling a massive hell swarm of infernal creatures like a plague of ravenous locusts hungry to devour the sun and enshroud the Earth in permanent midnight.

"VERY SOON OUR GREAT FATHER WILL SET THE EARTH ON FIRE. UNLEASHING THE ETERNAL BAT WHICH WILL DESTROY THE STARS AND MANKIND."

ANCIENT GUARANI PROPHECY
SOUTH AMERICAN FRAGMENT

VIEW REPORTS

DSP CRNT ACTIVE | HOST IP 10.0.92.256 | NO H/E SYNC | WX 40

SUPERSPECIES STATISTICS

MONARCH DESIGNATION: **SPIRIT TIGER**

CRYPTOZOOLOGICAL CLASSIFICATION: **TIGRIS SPIRITUS**

LENGTH: **15 FEET**

CLASSIFICATION: **UNKNOWN**

SUB-DIVISION: **UNKNOWN**

PREDATION: **UNKNOWN**

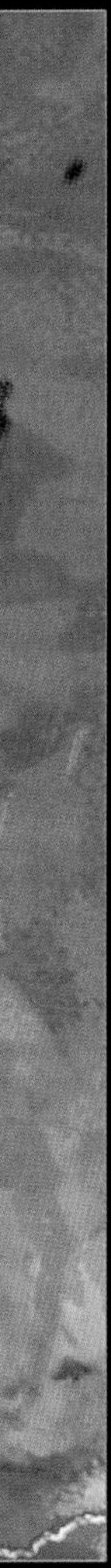

CREATURE PROFILE

THE REALITY

One of the most elegant, ethereal and mysterious creatures we have encountered upon the island, the Spirit Tiger was thought by many in our party to be a hallucination on first sighting. At one with the forest, the serrated stripes running the length of its body are composed of epidermal leaves that shimmer in the soft breezes of the higher peaks. When drawing closer to observe the Spirit Tiger, our entire party experienced a number of unusual physical phenomena, including dizziness, euphoria, and the ability to hear the creature's heart, audibly beating at the center of our heads. Iwi markings show a deep reverence for the Spirit Tiger, giving it a name that roughly translates as "Majesty of the Winds".

THREAT ANALYSIS

THE CREATURE'S PREDATION AND BREEDING PATTERNS REMAIN AN ELUSIVE MYSTERY.

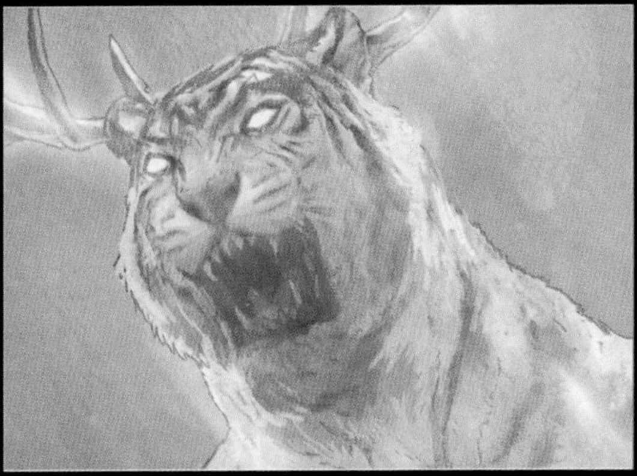

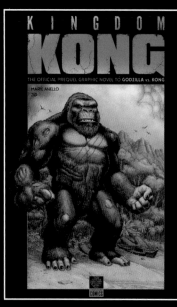
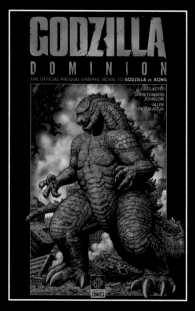

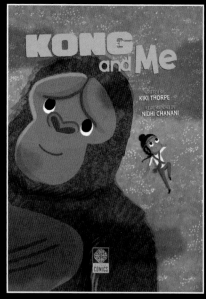